The Garden Entertaining Cookbook

The Garden Entertaining Cookbook

recipes and menus
for casual dining outdoors

Barbara Scott-Goodman
and Mary Goodbody

Photographs by Michael Grimm

CHRONICLE BOOKS
SAN FRANCISCO

Library of Congress Cataloging-in-Publication Data:

Scott-Goodman, Barbara
    The garden entertaining cookbook: recipes and menus for casual dining outdoors/
    by Barbara Scott-Goodman and Mary Goodbody:
    photographs by Michael Grimm.
        p. cm.
    Includes index.
    ISBN 0-8118-2956-1
    1. Outdoor cookery. 2. Entertaining. II. Goodbody, Mary. II. Title.
    TX823 .S3697 2001
    641.5'78-dc21   00-64455

Printed in China

Designed by Barbara Scott-Goodman
Food styling by Roscoe Betsill
Prop styling by Barbara Scott-Goodman

We wish to thank Broadway Panhandler, Fishs Eddy, and
Susan Kramer Design of New York City for the use of their wares.

Distributed in Canada by Raincoast Books
9050 Shaughnessy Street
Vancouver, BC V6P 6E5

10 9 8 7 6 5 4 3 2 1

Chronicle Books LLC
85 Second Street
San Francisco, California 94105

www.chroniclebooks.com

To Lester, Zan, and Isabelle,
and to my friend, Francis Donnelly.
—B.S.G.

To Laura, and to Gay, who encourages me in the garden.
—M.G.

ACKNOWLEDGMENTS

We would like to thank our friends and families for their enthusiastic support during the creation of this book. Many thanks to Bob Cornfield for all of his help, to Deborah Callen for recipe testing, and to Roscoe Betsill for his exquisite food styling. We are grateful to our good-natured dinner party guests who always happily sampled and commented on our many dishes. We also thank the talented people at Chronicle Books who helped make this book a reality.

A very special thanks to the gracious people who opened their homes and gardens to us. They are, Terry Hall and Donald Florence, Bronxville, New York; Heidi and David Johnston, Cross River, New York; Arlene Stewart, Katonah, New York; Stefan Sagmeister, New York City; Rick Livingston and Jim Brawders, Quogue, New York; Virginia and Jim Stier, Montauk, New York; and Joseph Keller and Ilsa Svendsen of the Garden of Ideas in Ridgefield, Connecticut.

And last, but not least, a great thank you to Michael Grimm, who always found the shot and made such wonderful photographs.

contents

INTRODUCTION   9

appetizers & cocktails

HERBED GOAT CHEESE SPREAD   15
ROASTED VEGETABLE CAPONATA
    WITH PITA CRISPS   16
HERBED OLIVES   18
TUNA TARTARE TOASTS   20
SCALLOP SEVICHE   21
SMOKED SALMON AND DILL
    DEVILED EGGS   22
VEGETABLE GARDEN BRUSCHETTA   23
JERSEY TOMATO SALSA   24
TOMATO-MANGO SALSA   26
CORN AND CHERRY TOMATO SALSA   26
BLACK BEAN SALSA   27

CHAMPAGNE-RASPBERRY COCKTAILS   28
VODKA-LIME SEA BREEZES   29
FROSTY MARGARITAS   29
SUMMER SANGRIA   30

soups

ICED CUCUMBER SOUP WITH YOGURT
    AND DILL   35
CHILLED AVOCADO SOUP   36
SPICY YELLOW TOMATO GAZPACHO   37
SUMMER BORSCHT   38
COLD MINTED PEA SOUP   40

BRAISED FENNEL SOUP   42
GRILLED SHRIMP AND
    CORN CHOWDER   44
OYSTER, LEEK, AND SCALLION SOUP   46

breads, sandwiches & pizza

GRILLED GARLIC-HERB BREAD   51
ROSEMARY FOCACCIA   52
SOUR CREAM CORNBREAD   54
SOFT-SHELL CRAB SANDWICHES   56
GRILLED CHICKEN AND BASIL
    MAYONNAISE SANDWICHES   58
GRILLED HAMBURGERS WITH
    RED ONION SAUCE   60
GRILLED LAMB BURGERS WITH COOL
    CUCUMBER SAUCE   62
GRILLED LATE-HARVEST PIZZA   65

main courses

GRILLED CHICKEN BREASTS WITH
    CHOPPED AVOCADO SALAD   71
GRILLED CORNISH GAME HENS WITH
    MINT SAUCE   73
SPICY SOUTHWESTERN-STYLE GRILLED
    FLANK STEAK   76
GRILLED VEAL CHOPS WITH WILD
    MUSHROOM SAUCE   78

GRILLED PORK-AND-PINEAPPLE KABOBS
WITH SCALLIONS 81
GRILLED LAMB CHOPS WITH MINTED
MANGO CHUTNEY 83
MIXED GRILL OF SAUSAGES WITH
TARRAGON-MUSTARD SAUCE 84
ROASTED HALIBUT WITH
PARSLEY-LEMON SAUCE 85
POACHED SALMON SALAD WITH
MUSTARD DRESSING 86
FISH FRY WITH HERBED
TARTAR SAUCE 88
GRILLED SALADE NIÇOISE WITH
FRESH GARDEN VEGETABLES 91
FETTUCCINE WITH SAUTÉED CHERRY
TOMATOES AND BASIL 93
ROASTED RED PEPPERS STUFFED
WITH FRESH CORN AND ZUCCHINI 94

salads & side dishes

HERBED POTATO SALAD 99
BASMATI RICE SALAD WITH FRESH
PEAS, CORN, AND CHIVES 100
TOMATO AND MIXED BASIL SALAD 102
CELERY ROOT AND CABBAGE SLAW 104
SNOW PEA–ORANGE SALAD 105
GRILLED PORTOBELLO MUSHROOM
SALAD WITH HERBED GOAT CHEESE 106
GRILLED SHRIMP SALAD 108
CRABMEAT SALAD WITH
HEIRLOOM TOMATOES 110
HARICOTS VERTS WITH
PARSLEY-PECAN PESTO 111

GRILLED CORN WITH
CILANTRO-CUMIN BUTTER 113
STEAMED MIXED VEGETABLES WITH
LEMON-HERB VINAIGRETTE 114
WARM LENTILS AND
SAUTÉED SPINACH 117

desserts & drinks

SUMMER BERRY SHORTCAKE 121
SOUR CREAM AND LEMON POUND
CAKE WITH WARM RHUBARB SAUCE 122
ORANGE ANGEL FOOD CAKE WITH
FRESH BERRIES AND
WHIPPED CREAM 125
BUFFALO BAY APPLE CRISP 126
PEAR COBBLER 128
WARM CRÊPES WITH SUMMER
BLUEBERRIES AND PEACHES 130
FRESH BERRY CROSTADA 133
MARBLED CHOCOLATE–CREAM
CHEESE BROWNIES 135
LAURA'S LEMON COOKIES 136
LEMON-LIME SORBET 137

ICED MINT AND LEMON VERBENA TEA 138
ICED ORANGE AND CLOVE TEA 139
ICED STRAWBERRY-LEMON TEA 139
FRESH–SQUEEZED LEMONADE 141
SPARKLING LIMEADE 141

INDEX 142

TABLE OF EQUIVALENTS 144

introduction

When the first green shoots appear in the garden amid the March mud and pockets of snow, we know something wonderful is beginning. During the next weeks, despite some impossibly unpleasant weather, other shoots appear, shoving up through the earth with the tenacity of a New York pedestrian. To the casual observer, spring begins slowly, but from its onset the garden works hard. To the gardener, early, wet spring is almost more exciting than May and June, which is when the show begins in earnest.

May and June are splashy times indeed. Daffodils, tulips, violets, and bleeding hearts give way to irises, evening primrose, phlox, Shasta daisies, and all sorts of fragrant roses. Herbs leaf out, tomato plants start to grow tall, lettuces are harvested, garlic put up soft green shoots, and beans climb up the pole on their way to the sun.

Until May, time spent in the garden is solitary. It's a time for muddy gloves and tools, seedlings and mulch. When the spring weather turns warm, the garden becomes communal. We invite friends and family to enjoy it, to drink in the gentle beauty of our flowers and the robust greenness of the vegetables. We put tables on decks and patios, colorful cushions on sturdy chairs, and roll out grills. To delight the senses, we arrange pots overflowing with petunias and impatiens or fragrant, aromatic herbs. Ice clinks in glasses filled with Frosty Margaritas or Summer Sangria, and we serve simple, fresh-tasting foods such as Roasted Vegetable Caponata with Pita Crisps, Herbed Olives, and Vegetable Garden Bruschetta. Chicken cooked on the grill is delicious, whether it's Grilled Chicken with Chopped Avocado Salad or Grilled Chicken and Basil Mayonnaise Sandwiches. So are Grilled Hamburgers with Red Onion Sauce, Spicy Southwestern-Style Grilled Flank Steak, and Grilled Lamb Chops with Minted Mango Chutney. Vibrantly colored spring and summer side dishes range from Snow Pea–Orange Salad to Haricots Verts with Parsley-Pecan Pesto. Desserts are easy and frosty, such as Lemon-Lime Sorbet, or rustic baked affairs bursting with bubbling fruit—Pear Cobbler and Buffalo Bay Apple Crisp.

Whether we host a large party in the garden or gather a few close friends for a lazy evening, it's the place we want to be as summer's glory marches towards autumn's majesty. Even when the weather cools, the afternoon sun is warm enough to enjoy—an amble through the vegetable garden is more inspiring than all the cookbooks on the shelf. It's time to cook from the garden.

Think Seasonally, Cook Locally

We believe with all our hearts that the best food comes from our own backyards. This may be our own garden or our neighbor's, or more likely, a nearby farmer's field or orchard, where the vegetables are picked on the day they are sold at the farmers' market. The fresher the peach, plum, squash, cucumber, or tomato, the better its flavor. It's still close enough to the earth and rain to taste indescribably fresh and sweet.

Even greengrocers deep in the city, and supermarkets sprawling in the suburbs tend to have better-tasting produce in the summer and early fall. Some market their food as being "locally grown." Buy this if you can. It's a good way to support your local farmers, insure the stability of a green belt near you, and guarantee that the food you serve will taste as good and be as wholesome as possible.

A Tranquil Place

Everyone loves being outside when the weather is fine, so during the warm summer months the garden is the ideal place to entertain. The flowers and vegetables offer a splendid backdrop, children can race around while the adults visit, and no one really cares if food gets dropped on the lawn or a drink spills on the flagstones.

If you plan your meal around what is freshest and in season at the moment, no one will be disappointed. Use our recipes as inspiration for parties and family gatherings. Use your own backyard, deck, or patio as the setting and you will find that there's no better place than the garden to enjoy the happiest things in life.

appetizers & cocktails

Who loves a garden still his Eden keeps,
Perennial pleasures plants,
and wholesome harvests reaps.

—AMOS BRONSON ALCOTT

HERBED GOAT CHEESE SPREAD

Makes about 1 cup

This tangy, goat cheese spread is made with fresh tarragon, parsley, and scallions, but you can substitute just about any fresh herb from the garden. The possibilities are endless. We mix the goat cheese with drained plain yogurt, which gives it a lovely consistency. For a delightful hors d'oeuvre to accompany drinks before dinner, serve the spread with grilled bread and an assortment of olives.

6 ounces plain nonfat yogurt
6 ounces mild goat cheese, at room temperature
2 teaspoons finely chopped fresh tarragon
2 tablespoons finely chopped fresh flat-leaf parsley
2 tablespoons finely minced scallions, white and green parts
Salt and freshly ground black pepper

1. Line a sieve with a coffee filter and place it over a bowl. Spoon the yogurt into the filter and let it drain for about 1 hour at room temperature, or overnight in the refrigerator.

2. In a medium bowl, gently mash the goat cheese with a fork to soften. Add the tarragon, parsley, and scallions and work them in with the fork. Season to taste with salt and pepper, mashing to make a smooth, well-blended spread.

3. Add the yogurt and mix until well blended. If you are not serving at once, cover and refrigerate. The spread can be made up to 2 days ahead of time. Bring it to room temperature before serving.

ROASTED VEGETABLE CAPONATA WITH PITA CRISPS

Serves 12 to 15 (makes about 6 cups of caponata)

Here is one of those dishes that you will want to make often. Based mainly on eggplant, the caponata mingles sweet, golden raisins with the traditional Mediterranean flavors of tomatoes, capers, olives, and fresh herbs. We recommend serving the spread on Pita Crisps (recipe follows), but if you prefer, use your favorite crackers or bread.

½ cup golden raisins
¾ cup dry red wine
3 medium eggplants, peeled and cut into ½-inch-thick slices
2 large red onions, cut into ½-inch-thick slices
½ cup olive oil
1 can (28 ounces) plum tomatoes
3 tablespoons drained capers
1 cup chopped kalamata olives
1 jar (5½ ounces) pitted Spanish olives, drained
1 jalapeño pepper, seeded and minced
⅓ cup balsamic vinegar
½ cup shredded fresh basil leaves
½ cup finely chopped fresh flat-leaf parsley
Salt and freshly ground black pepper
Pita Crisps (recipe follows), crackers, or bread

   1. Preheat the oven to 400°F.
   2. Put the raisins in a small saucepan and cover with the wine. Bring to a simmer over medium heat and cook for about 3 minutes. Set aside for at least 15 minutes to give the raisins time to plump.
   3. Brush the eggplant and onion slices with olive oil and arrange in separate roasting pans in single layers, but don't worry if the slices overlap. Roast, turning once, for 25 to 30 minutes, until soft and lightly browned.

▲

MIDSUMMER DINNER
IN THE GARDEN

*roasted vegetable
caponata*
•
pita crisps
•
*grilled lamb chops with
minted mango chutney*
•
herbed potato salad
•
green salad
•
fresh berry crostada
•
merlot

4. Meanwhile, drain the juice from the tomatoes into a large mixing bowl. Chop the tomatoes and add to the bowl. Stir in the plumped raisins and any wine still in the pan, the capers, the kalamata and Spanish olives, and jalapeño.

5. Chop the roasted eggplant and onion into coarse chunks and add to the tomato mixture. Add the vinegar, basil, and parsley and season to taste with salt and pepper. Toss gently, cover, and let the mixture mellow for 6 to 8 hours or overnight in the refrigerator. The caponata will keep for up to 1 week in the refrigerator.

6. Before serving, taste and adjust the seasonings, if necessary. Serve at room temperature with Pita Crisps, crackers, or bread.

PITA CRISPS

Makes about 12 dozen crisps

Nothing could be easier than baking these little pita wedges and they are much better than store-bought crackers for serving with our caponata or with any other vegetable spread. They are also terrific with bean dips and all kinds of salsa. If you prefer, cut the wedges wider than we do.

¾ cup olive oil
2 teaspoons paprika
Ten 6-inch pita pockets
Kosher salt

1. Preheat the oven to 350°F.

2. In a small bowl, stir together the olive oil and paprika.

3. Using a sharp knife, halve the pitas horizontally. Brush the rough sides of the pitas with the paprika oil and season generously with salt.

4. Cut each pita half into 7 or 8 wedges and arrange them in single layers on large, ungreased baking sheets. Bake in the middle of the oven for about 10 minutes, or until lightly browned and crisp. Cool on wire racks before serving. The pita crisps can be made up to 2 days ahead of time and stored in resealable plastic bags at room temperature.

HERBED OLIVES

Makes about 1 pint

Try these olives with other fresh herbs from the garden such as thyme, tarragon, or marjoram. Increasing numbers of supermarkets offer a selection of cured olives, sold in small tubs so that you can mix and match your favorites. We like to marinate a combination of green olives, but you might want to try black olives or a mixture. The olive oil will congeal when it's refrigerated, so be sure to let the olives sit at room temperature before serving.

4 teaspoons black or multicolored peppercorns
1 tablespoon crushed fresh rosemary
1 tablespoon crushed red pepper flakes
1 teaspoon fennel seeds
3 cups (about 1 pound) mixed brine-cured green olives,
*   drained if necessary*
1½ cups extra-virgin olive oil
2 bay leaves
2 cloves garlic, crushed

1. In a small bowl, mix together the peppercorns, rosemary, pepper flakes, and fennel seeds. Add the olives and toss to coat and mix. Add the olive oil, bay leaves, and garlic, toss again to coat, cover and refrigerate for at least 2 hours and up to 2 weeks. Let the olives come to room temperature before serving.

TUNA TARTARE TOASTS

Serves 8

The key to successful tuna tartare is "sushi-quality" tuna, which is the freshest and best you can buy. It may cost a little more than other tuna, and you may have to search for a market that sells it, but it's worth it for this recipe. Plus, you don't need much. Chop the tuna on a pristine work surface with a clean knife, and once it's tossed with the other ingredients, let it mellow for no longer than two hours. Otherwise, its texture will soften. The fresh flavors of the tuna, herbs, and shallots speak of warm summer days and all that is good about outdoor entertaining.

1 pound sushi-quality fresh tuna
2 tablespoons finely chopped fresh cilantro
2 tablespoons finely chopped flat-leaf parsley
1 tablespoon minced shallot
1 teaspoon finely grated fresh ginger
2 teaspoons olive oil
Salt and freshly ground black pepper
2 teaspoons fresh lime juice
2 medium cucumbers, sliced paper thin
1 small red onion, sliced paper thin
32 crustless toast points, approximately 2 inches at the base
2 tablespoons capers, drained

1. Using a sharp knife, dice the tuna as finely as possible. Transfer to a medium bowl and add the cilantro, parsley, shallot, ginger, and olive oil. Mix gently and season to taste with salt and pepper. Continue mixing gently until the ingredients are thoroughly combined. Cover and refrigerate up to but no longer than 2 hours.

2. When ready to serve, gently toss the lime juice with the tuna. To assemble, arrange the cucumbers and then the onions on the toast points. Spoon the tuna tartare over the onions and top with a few capers. Serve immediately.

SCALLOP SEVICHE

Serves 6

When making seviche, use the freshest scallops you can find; the integrity of the dish will be compromised if you don't begin with the best there is. Don't let this warning fool you into thinking that the scallops will be eaten raw. The acid—in this case the lemon juice— actually breaks down the fibers and connective tissue in the scallops, accomplishing the same end as cooking. We love serving this salad as a first course or light meal. The fresh corn does not need to be cooked if it's young and tender; if frozen, steam or boil the corn for a few minutes.

1½ pounds bay scallops, or sea scallops, halved
½ cup fresh lemon juice (2 to 3 lemons),
    plus extra for drizzling (optional)
¼ cup extra-virgin olive oil
1 cup fresh or frozen and thawed yellow corn kernels
¼ cup finely chopped red onion
1 pint cherry tomatoes, halved if large
Salt and freshly ground white pepper
1 ripe Haas avocado
½ cup loosely packed fresh basil leaves

1. In a small, deep glass or ceramic bowl, toss the scallops and the ½ cup lemon juice. Cover and refrigerate for at least 4 hours, and no longer than 6 hours.

2. About 40 minutes before serving, transfer the scallops and juices to a mixing bowl. Add the olive oil, corn, red onion, and 6 to 8 of the cherry tomatoes, and stir gently. Season with salt and pepper, cover, and refrigerate for about 30 minutes, until ready to serve.

3. Spoon the seviche on a platter. Halve the avocado, remove the pit, peel, and slice into wedges. Garnish the platter with avocado slices, the remaining cherry tomatoes, and the basil leaves. Drizzle extra lemon juice over the salad, if desired.

if you can, buy fresh eggs from a farmers' market or store that sells eggs from a farm nearby. The fresher the egg, the better the flavor. Grades given eggs by the industry refer to fresh-ness, too: AA eggs are the best choice. For deviled eggs, we suggest eggs as fresh as can be, either white or brown shelled. If you prefer, vary the filling by adding chopped anchovies or capers, finely shredded crabmeat, minced red peppers or red onions, and any fresh herb that tastes good to you.

SMOKED SALMON AND DILL DEVILED EGGS

Serves 6

These eggs are a mystery to us. Our guests say they "never eat eggs," but these are the first to disappear from a summer buffet table. The addition of smoked salmon to the stuffing clearly makes them irresistible.

6 large eggs
2 ounces smoked salmon, finely chopped (about ¼ cup)
2 tablespoons finely chopped red onion
2 tablespoons minced fresh dill
Fresh lemon juice to taste
½ cup mayonnaise
1 tablespoon Dijon mustard
Freshly ground black pepper
12 dill sprigs, for garnish

1. Put the eggs in a large pot and cover with cold water. Bring to a gentle boil over medium-high heat. When the water just begins to boil, turn off the heat and cover the pot tightly. Let the eggs stand, covered, for 30 minutes. Drain and rinse under cold water. Pat dry and let cool.

2. When the eggs are cool enough to handle, peel and slice them in half lengthwise. Carefully scoop out the yolks and transfer them to a large mixing bowl. Set the egg whites aside on a platter. If necessary, slice a thin sliver from the rounded underside of each egg white so that they will sit on the platter.

3. Mash the yolks with a fork. Add the smoked salmon, red onion, dill, and lemon juice. Stir in the mayonnaise and mustard and mix well. Season with pepper to taste. Spoon the egg yolk mixture onto the egg white halves. Top each with a sprig of dill. The deviled eggs may be covered with plastic wrap and refrigerated for up to 3 hours before serving.

VEGETABLE GARDEN BRUSCHETTA

Serves 6

Nothing tastes quite like summer tomatoes. Pick them when they are plump and warm from the sun, mixing varieties and sizes (and colors, if possible) for this lovely, classic tomato salad. Use the fruitiest olive oil you have; sprinkle it with a little coarse salt to accentuate its flavor. Imported Parmesan, grated over the tomatoes in coarse shavings, makes a huge flavor statement (store-bought grated Parmesan really won't do).

1½ pounds ripe tomatoes (5 or 6 medium)
3 scallions, white and green parts, sliced
¼ cup shredded fresh basil leaves
1 clove garlic, minced
2 tablespoons balsamic or red wine vinegar
1 to 2 teaspoons fresh lemon juice
Salt and freshly ground black pepper
Twelve ½-inch-thick slices country-style bread, such as ciabatta
About ½ cup extra-virgin olive oil
Coarse salt for sprinkling
6 ounces Parmesan cheese

1. Core and halve the tomatoes. Chop them into ½ inch dice and transfer them and any escaped juices to a small, ceramic or glass bowl. Add the scallions, basil, garlic, vinegar, and lemon juice. Season to taste with salt and pepper, cover, and set aside at room temperature for at least 30 minutes and no longer than 2 hours. Stir gently several times to distribute the flavors. Just before serving, taste and adjust the seasoning.

2. Lightly toast the bread on both sides. Arrange the toasts on a platter and brush each slice with olive oil. Sprinkle each with a little coarse salt.

3. Spoon the tomato mixture on the toasts, distributing it evenly. Using a hand-held grater or small, sharp knife, shave or coarsely grate the Parmesan over the tomatoes. It is best if some of the cheese is in large, thin shards. Serve immediately.

SALSA

Translated from Spanish, salsa means "sauce," but so familiar is the term in English that few of us think of its Mexican roots when we make it.

We have devised recipes using the traditional tomatoes, but we have also included ingredients as diverse as mangoes, pineapple juice, black beans, and fresh corn. Some of our salsas are hot and spicy, others are cooler. We serve them with chips, but we also eat them with grilled or pan-seared fish and shrimp, chicken, pork, and beef. All the salsas on these pages can be made ahead of time. When covered and refrigerated, they keep for up to three days. They are very good served chilled, but we prefer them at cool room temperature.

JERSEY TOMATO SALSA

Make about 3 cups

2 large tomatoes, preferably Jersey beefsteaks, seeded and coarsely chopped
1 medium green bell pepper, seeded, deribbed, and diced
1 medium red bell pepper, seeded, deribbed, and diced
1 medium red onion, cut into ¼-inch dice
2 tablespoons olive oil
2 tablespoons chopped fresh flat-leaf parsley
2 tablespoons chopped fresh chives
1 teaspoon chili powder
Pinch of cayenne pepper
Salt and freshly ground black pepper

1. Combine the tomatoes, peppers, and onion in a large bowl. Add the olive oil and toss gently to mix.

2. Add the parsley, chives, chili powder, and cayenne, and toss gently. Season to taste with salt and pepper. Cover and refrigerate for at least 2 hours or until well chilled.

3. Serve chilled or at room temperature. The salsa will keep in the refrigerator for up to 3 days.

TOMATO-MANGO SALSA

Makes about 4 cups

4 plum tomatoes (about 1 pound), seeded and chopped into ¼-inch dice
3 small or 2 large ripe mangoes, peeled, pitted, and diced
1 medium red onion, finely chopped
1 medium red pepper, seeded, deribbed, and cut into ¼-inch dice
1 tablespoon plus 1 teaspoon minced garlic
1 teaspoon red pepper flakes
¼ cup chopped fresh cilantro
¼ cup pineapple juice
2 tablespoons distilled white vinegar
2 tablespoons fresh lime juice

1. Combine the tomatoes, mangoes, onion, pepper, garlic, pepper flakes, and cilantro in a large, glass or ceramic bowl, and mix gently.

2. In another large bowl, whisk together the pineapple juice, vinegar, and lime juice. Add to the tomato mixture and stir gently. Cover and refrigerate for at least 2 hours or until well chilled.

3. Serve chilled or at room temperature. The salsa will keep in the refrigerator for up to 3 days.

CORN AND CHERRY TOMATO SALSA

Makes about 4 cups

3 medium ears corn, husked
2 cups red and yellow cherry tomatoes, coarsely chopped
1 medium red bell pepper, seeded, deribbed, and diced
1 medium red onion, cut into ¼-inch dice
6 scallions, trimmed and minced
½ cup fresh cilantro
2 tablespoons balsamic vinegar
2 tablespoons fresh lime juice
2 teaspoons ground cumin

▲

COCKTAIL PARTY
ON THE DECK

*corn and cherry
tomato salsa*
•
black bean salsa nachos
•
*yellow and blue
corn chips*
•
*herbed goat
cheese spread*
•
herbed olives
•
assorted breads
•
beer & wine
•
summer sangria
•
frosty margaritas

1. Bring a large pot of water to a boil. Add the corn, return to the boil, and cook for 5 minutes. Lift the corn from the water and set aside to cool. When cool enough to handle, scrape the kernels off the cobs with a small, sharp knife, and transfer to a large bowl.

2. Add the tomatoes, pepper, onion, scallions, cilantro, vinegar, lime juice, and cumin and toss gently. Cover and set aside at room temperature for at least 1 hour, or cover and refrigerate for at least 2 hours or until well chilled.

3. Serve chilled or at room temperature. The salsa will keep in the refrigerator for up to 3 days.

BLACK BEAN SALSA

Makes about 3 cups

2 cups canned black beans, drained and rinsed
1 large tomato, seeded and coarsely chopped
2 cloves garlic, minced
2 jalapeños, seeded and minced
2 scallions, white and green parts thinly sliced
1 small red onion, chopped into ¼-inch dice
2 tablespoons chopped fresh cilantro
1 teaspoon ground cumin
1 teaspoon chili powder
1 tablespoon olive oil
1½ teaspoons red wine vinegar
1½ teaspoons fresh lemon juice
Salt and freshly ground black pepper

1. Combine all the ingredients except the salt and pepper in a large bowl. Stir gently. Season to taste with salt and pepper.

2. Cover and refrigerate for at least 2 hours or until well chilled.

3. Serve chilled or at room temperature. The salsa will keep in the refrigerator for up to 3 days.

TOMATOES

tomatoes are a favorite crop of most gardeners. Whether you grow them from commercial seeds, bought from a seed-saver company (for old-fashioned varieties, often called heirloom tomatoes), or from seedlings bought at the nursery, with little effort, you will have a bountiful harvest. They require lots of sun, plenty of legroom, ample water, and staking as they grow. Some of the most popular are Better Boy, Celebrity, Big Boy, Beefmaster, and Roma. Sun Gold and Sweet 100s are very good cherry tomatoes, suitable for the garden or pots.

COCKTAILS

Savoring a glass of excellent wine in a quiet garden is a relaxing way to end a busy day. But there are times when you and your guests are in the mood for more festive alcoholic refreshment. These are the occasions for fruity sangria, elegant Champagne-Raspberry Cocktails, tart Vodka-Lime Sea Breezes, and "blender drinks"—that we have come to associate with warm weather and parties—such as our Frosty Margaritas. When a drink calls for fresh fruit, we like to take advantage of what's best and in season, which explains why, for instance, we add peaches and strawberries to the sangria.

   If possible, serve these cocktails in the appropriate glasses. Cocktail glasses, which are stemmed and have wide bowls, are best for icy drinks made in the blender. The sangria and sea breezes should be poured into tall glasses, while the Champagne cocktails should be served in fluted Champagne glasses.

CHAMPAGNE-RASPBERRY COCKTAILS

Serves 6

1 cup fresh raspberries, plus 6 plump berries for garnish
3 tablespoons crème de cassis
2 tablespoons superfine sugar
One bottle (750 ml) Champagne or sparkling wine, chilled

   1. Put the raspberries, crème de cassis, and sugar in a blender, and process until smooth. Refrigerate for 30 minutes.

   2. Spoon 2 heaping teaspoons of the purée into each champagne glass. Slowly pour the wine over the raspberry purée, giving the bubbles a chance to subside a little before filling the glasses. Garnish each glass with a raspberry, and serve at once.

VODKA-LIME SEA BREEZES

Serves 6

3 cups cranberry juice
⅔ cup grapefruit juice
Juice of 1 lime
1 cup vodka
Lime slices, for garnish

   1. Pour the cranberry juice, grapefruit juice, lime juice, and vodka into a large pitcher and stir well. Serve poured over ice in tall glasses, garnished with lime slices.

FROSTY MARGARITAS

Serves 6

1 cup tequila
⅓ cup Triple Sec
¾ cup fresh lime juice, 6 to 8 limes
Ice
Coarse salt for coating glasses
1 lime, quartered
Thin lime slices, for garnish

   1. Put 6 sturdy cocktail glasses into the freezer to frost them.
   2. Pour the tequila, Triple Sec, and lime juice into a blender. Add ice to fill the container, and blend until the ice is crushed.
   3. Spread the salt on a flat plate. Rub the rims of the frosted glassed with the quartered lime, and then dip the rims in the salt to coat.
   4. Pour the margaritas into the glasses, and serve at once, garnished with lime slices.

▲

EARLY SUMMER
SUNDAY LUNCH

*champagne-raspberry
cocktails*

•

tuna tartare toasts

•

cold minted pea soup

•

*poached salmon salad
with mustard dressing*

•

*sour cream and lemon
pound cake with
warm rhubarb sauce*

SUMMER SANGRIA

Serves 6

SYRUP:

1 cup sugar
½ cup water
Zest of 1 orange
Zest of 1 lemon
1 cinnamon stick

SANGRIA:

One bottle (750 ml) full-bodied red wine, such as Côtes du Rhône
¼ cup brandy
½ orange, thinly sliced
½ lemon, thinly sliced
1 peach, peeled, pitted, and thinly sliced (optional)
8 fresh strawberries (optional)

1. To make the syrup: Mix together the sugar, water, orange zest, and lemon zest in a saucepan and bring to a boil over high heat. Reduce the heat, add the cinnamon stick, and simmer, stirring with a wooden spoon, for about 5 minutes, until the sugar dissolves. Strain into a lidded glass jar or similar container. Discard the cinnamon stick. Cool, cover, and refrigerate.

2. To make the sangria: Pour the wine, brandy, and ¼ cup of the syrup into a pitcher; reserve the remaining syrup for later batches of sangria. Add the orange and lemon slices and the peach and strawberries, if using, and stir. Refrigerate for 2 to 3 hours or until ready to serve. Pour over ice in tall glasses.

soups

My garden will never make me famous,
I'm a horticultural ignoramus,
I can't tell a stringbean from a soybean,
Or even a girl bean from a boy bean.

—OGDEN NASH

ICED CUCUMBER SOUP WITH YOGURT AND DILL

Serves 6 to 8

Cucumbers are easy to find all year long, but they taste best in the summer, particularly if they are homegrown or bought from a local farmer. These watery vegetables are usually served raw in salads or pickled. Here we cook them for a soup with a softer flavor than similar dishes.

3½ pounds cucumbers (5 to 6 medium), peeled, seeded, and chopped
1 small onion, sliced
3 tablespoons cider vinegar
3 tablespoons coarsely chopped fresh dill
8 to 9 cups chicken stock, preferably homemade
½ cup heavy cream or milk
Salt and freshly ground white pepper
1 to 1½ cups plain yogurt
Chopped fresh dill for garnish
1 cucumber, thinly sliced, for garnish

1. In a stockpot, combine the cucumbers, onion, vinegar, and dill. Add the stock and bring to a boil, stirring, over high heat. Lower the heat to medium-low and simmer, partially covered, for about 30 minutes, until the cucumbers are very soft. Set aside to cool until barely warm.

2. Purée the soup in a food processor fitted with a metal blade or a blender (if using a blender, do this in batches). Transfer to a bowl and stir in the cream. Season to taste with salt and pepper. Cover and chill for at least 4 hours or overnight.

3. Spoon the yogurt into shallow, chilled, soup bowls. Adjust the seasonings and then ladle the soup over the yogurt. Garnish with dill and cucumber slices and serve.

CUCUMBER COOL

this mild-flavored, watery vegetable is easy to find in markets and greengrocers and is at its best in the warm months. Look for slender, green cukes—the giants are full of tasteless seeds—and slice them for salads or sandwiches, chop them for dips, or use them to make soup. The most common cucumber is the smooth cuke, although it's also easy to find bumpy Kirbys (also called pickling cukes) and long seedless cucumbers (also called English or hot-house). Home gardeners grow other varieties, which rarely show up for retail sale but taste terrific.

CHILLED AVOCADO SOUP

Serves 6

When the weather is too hot to cook, try this raw soup made with avocados, chicken stock, and a few fresh basil leaves from the garden. We recommend dark green Haas avocados for their nutty, rich flavor and silken texture, although larger, paler Fuerte are very good, too. Both are in season in midsummer. Select unblemished and perfectly ripe fruit that yields when you press it with your fingertips, like peaches do.

4 large ripe avocados, peeled and pitted
¼ cup plus 2 tablespoons fresh lemon juice
3 cups plain lowfat yogurt
3 cups chicken stock, preferably homemade
¼ cup finely chopped fresh flat-leaf parsley
4 large fresh basil leaves, thinly sliced
Salt and freshly ground black pepper
1 red bell pepper, seeded, deribbed, and finely chopped, for garnish
1 yellow bell pepper, seeded, deribbed, and finely chopped, for garnish

DINNER
ON THE PORCH

chilled avocado soup
•
*grilled cornish game hens
with mint sauce*
•
*basmati rice salad
with fresh peas, corn,
and chives*
•
lemon-lime sorbet
•
mâcon-villages

1. Coarsely chop the avocados and put them in a large bowl. Add the lemon juice and toss gently to coat. Add the yogurt, chicken stock, parsley, and basil. Season to taste with salt and pepper and stir well.

2. Transfer the mixture to a food processor fitted with a metal blade and process until very smooth, scraping down the sides of the work bowl if necessary. You may have to do this in batches. Pour the soup into a large nonreactive bowl. If the soup seems too thick, add a bit of stock or water. Cover and refrigerate for 2 to 3 hours, or until chilled.

3. Ladle the soup into chilled soup bowls. Sprinkle with the diced red and yellow peppers, and serve immediately.

SPICY YELLOW TOMATO GAZPACHO

Serves 6

Refreshing and spicy, this version of gazpacho will win raves from your guests. If yellow tomatoes are unavailable or in short supply, use red ones or a combination of red and yellow. Serve cold, topped with home-made croutons and fresh cilantro.

GAZPACHO:

4 large yellow tomatoes, cored and cut into small wedges
2 medium red bell peppers, seeded, deribbed, and finely chopped
2 medium yellow bell peppers, seeded, deribbed, and finely chopped
2 medium cucumbers, peeled, seeded, and coarsely chopped
1 medium red onion, coarsely chopped
2 cloves garlic, thinly sliced
2 cups chicken stock, preferably homemade
⅓ cup balsamic or sherry vinegar
Dash of Tabasco sauce
Pinch of cayenne pepper
2 tablespoons capers, drained
Salt and freshly ground black pepper

CROUTONS:

3 tablespoons olive oil
2 cups day-old ½-inch bread cubes

½ cup chopped fresh cilantro leaves, for garnish

  1. To make the gazpacho: Put all of the ingredients in a large bowl and stir to mix well.
  2. Transfer half of the mixture to a blender or a food processor fitted with a metal blade and process until smooth. Return to the bowl and mix well. Taste and adjust the seasonings, if necessary. Cover and refrigerate for at least 4 hours, or overnight.

continued

3. To make the croutons: Heat the oil in a large skillet over medium heat. Add the bread cubes and toss to coat with the oil. Reduce the heat to low and sauté the bread, stirring frequently, for 15 to 20 minutes, until light golden brown. Remove from the heat to cool.

4. Ladle the soup into shallow, chilled soup bowls. Top with croutons, season with salt and pepper, and sprinkle with cilantro.

SUMMER BORSCHT

Serves 6 to 8

Late in the summer, when beets taste their earthy best, we make this easy, bright-red borscht. Not all beets are red; if you select golden, pink, or white beets instead, the borscht may not have its crimson hue, but its flavor will still be excellent. Make sure an inch or more of the stem is intact on each bulb. Otherwise, they may be dry and tough.

3 pounds medium beets with stems (about 6), trimmed, peeled,
*   and sliced into ½-inch-thick slices*
1 large tomato, peeled and coarsely chopped
1 medium red or yellow bell pepper, seeded, deribbed,
*   and coarsely chopped*
4 cups water
2 cups chicken or vegetable stock, preferably homemade
1 tablespoon safflower or canola oil
1 large red onion, coarsely chopped
4 scallions, white part trimmed and minced
½ cup finely chopped fresh flat-leaf parsley
⅓ cup fresh orange juice
Salt and freshly ground black pepper
Sour cream for garnish
Snipped fresh chives, for garnish

1. In a large pot, combine the beets, tomato, bell pepper, water, and stock and bring to a boil over high heat. Reduce the heat and simmer, partially covered, for 35 to 40 minutes, or until the vegetables are tender. Remove from the heat and set aside to cool.

2. Meanwhile, heat the oil in a small sauté pan over medium heat. Add the onion and scallions, cover, and cook, stirring occasionally, for about 10 minutes, or until tender. Stir the parsley into the vegetables just before removing from the heat. Stir the contents of the pan into the beet mixture.

3. Drain the beet and onion mixture over a large bowl and reserve the cooking liquid.

4. Transfer half of the vegetables to a food processor fitted with a metal blade and purée. With the motor running, pour 1½ cups of the cooking liquid through the feed tube. When smooth, pour into a non-reactive bowl. Repeat with the remaining vegetables and 1½ cups of the cooking liquid. Discard the remaining cooking liquid.

5. Stir the orange juice into the soup. Season to taste with salt and pepper and mix well. Cover and refrigerate for 2 to 3 hours, or until well chilled.

6. Stir the soup and adjust the seasoning, if necessary. Ladle into chilled soup bowls. Garnish each serving with a dollop of sour cream and a sprinkling of chives. Serve at once.

BEETS

While beets are delicious in borscht, you can also use them in side dishes, salads, and pickles. Easy to grow, you can harvest the beet tops in the spring and the bulbs in the fall. They like water, good sun (a little shade is okay), and light, sandy soil. When buying beets, look for all sizes, from the size of marbles to that of lemons, but be sure they are firm and smooth with about an inch of stem attached, which prevents drying. Not all are red: look for pink, white, and golden.

COLD MINTED PEA SOUP

Serves 6

If you grow English peas, the common green peas in a pod, or if your local farmers' market sells them, use them for this light, easy soup. If not, frozen peas will work well. Shelling fresh peas is a pleasant pastime and a way to get in touch with the goodness of fresh vegetables.

2 tablespoons olive oil
4 to 5 scallions, white and green parts, finely chopped
4 cups shelled fresh peas or frozen peas (20 ounces)
¼ cup coarsely chopped fresh mint leaves
6 cups chicken or vegetable stock, preferably homemade
Salt and freshly ground black pepper
½ cup half-and-half
Plain yogurt, for garnish
2 tablespoons minced fresh mint leaves, for garnish
1 scallion, white and green parts, thinly sliced, for garnish

1. In a large pot, heat the olive oil over medium-high heat. Add the scallions and cook, stirring, for 1 to 2 minutes, until softened. Add the peas and mint leaves and cook, stirring, for about 5 minutes, until softened and fragrant. Add the stock and bring to a boil over high heat. Reduce the heat and simmer for 15 to 20 minutes. Season to taste with salt and pepper. Let the soup cool to room temperature.

2. Transfer the soup in batches to a food processor or blender and process until smooth. Strain through a sieve into a pot, pushing hard with the back of a spoon to extract as much liquid as possible. Alternatively, purée the soup using a food mill. Discard the solids.

3. Stir in the half-and-half, adjust the seasonings, cover, and refrigerate for at least 2 hours until chilled.

4. Stir well before ladling into chilled bowls. Garnish each serving with a dollop of yogurt, minced mint leaves, and sliced scallions.

BRAISED FENNEL SOUP

Serves 6 to 8

Fennel, that beautiful, pale-green vegetable, is related to both carrots and parsnips, but its anise flavor and crunchy texture are entirely its own. When buying fennel, look for bulbs with their stalks intact, complete within the feathery fronds. Press the flesh of the bulb to test for freshness; it should feel firm and resist gentle pressure. If it's soft or pulpy, pass up. Fennel, also known as finocchio, may be sautéed, roasted, or grilled, but our favorite method of cooking is braising. We like to braise it in the oven with other vegetables until very tender before puréeing it into a rich and aromatic soup.

2 medium fennel bulbs (about 1¼ pounds)
3 tablespoons olive oil
3 cloves garlic, thinly sliced
1 medium onion, peeled and coarsely chopped
1 medium Yukon Gold or other firm white potato, peeled and cubed
2 medium carrots, peeled and diced
8 sprigs fresh flat-leaf parsley
Pinch of dried thyme
2 tablespoons unsalted butter, cut into small pieces
6 cups chicken or vegetable stock, preferably homemade,
  or a mixture of stock and water
Salt and freshly ground black pepper
1 teaspoon Pernod liqueur
1 cup half-and half

   1. Preheat the oven to 350°F. Trim the feathery fronds from the fennel, chop them, and set aside. Core and halve or quarter the bulbs.
   2. Coat the bottom of a large roasting pan with the olive oil. Put the fennel bulbs, garlic, onion, potato, and carrots in the pan. Add the parsley sprigs and sprinkle with thyme. Dot with the butter and pour the stock over the vegetables. Season to taste with salt and pepper, cover the

pan tightly with aluminum foil, and roast for about 1 hour. Remove the foil and roast another 15 minutes, or until the vegetables are very tender. If the vegetables are dry, add a little more stock or water for the last 15 minutes of roasting. Let the vegetables cool in the pan.

3. Transfer the vegetables to a food processor fitted with a metal blade and purée until smooth. You will have to do this in batches. Put the purée in a large saucepan or stockpot and cook over medium-low heat. Stir in the Pernod and half-and-half and let the soup get as hot as possible without boiling. Adjust the seasoning and reheat gently, if necessary.

4. Ladle the soup into bowls, sprinkle with the chopped fennel fronds, and serve at once.

▲

LATE-SUMMER
LUNCH
IN THE GARDEN

braised fennel soup
•
*grilled salade niçoise
with fresh garden
vegetables*
•
strawberry ice cream
•
rosé
•
iced coffee

GRILLED SHRIMP AND CORN CHOWDER

Serves 6

It's amazing how a technique as simple as grilling the corn and shrimp enhances their already wonderful flavors, transforming this delicious soup into something truly special. The other ingredients provide their own fresh taste: garden tomatoes, sweet bell peppers, and a piquant jalapeño. Best of all, the summery chowder is a cinch to make.

2 tablespoons olive oil
1 small red onion, peeled and finely chopped
2 red bell peppers, seeded, deveined, and cut into 1-inch pieces
1 jalapeño pepper, stemmed, seeded, and finely minced
4 cups chicken stock, preferably homemade
2 cups water
1 cup chopped fresh tomatoes (2 medium tomatoes)
1 pound medium-sized shrimp, shelled and deveined (about 30 shrimp)
4 medium-sized ears corn, husked
Corn or canola oil, for brushing
2 teaspoons white vinegar
Salt and freshly ground black pepper
3 tablespoons minced fresh flat-leaf parsley, for garnish

1. Prepare a gas or charcoal grill. Lightly spray the grill rack with vegetable oil spray to prevent sticking. Heat the coals until very hot, covered with a thin layer of white ash and glowing deep red.

2. Heat the olive oil in a stockpot. Add the onion, red pepper, and jalapeño, and cook over low heat for about 10 minutes, until softened. Add the stock, water, and tomatoes. Bring to a boil, reduce the heat to medium, cover, and simmer for 10 to 15 minutes. Remove from the heat.

3. Thread the shrimp on skewers. Brush the shrimp and each ear of corn with a bit of the oil.

continued

4. Grill the shrimp for 2 to 3 minutes per side until just cooked through and pink. Remove the shrimp from the skewers and set aside. Grill the corn, turning often, for about 10 minutes, until lightly browned. When cool enough to handle, cut the kernels off the cobs with a sharp knife.

5. Stir the vinegar and the corn kernels into the soup. Season to taste with salt and pepper. Heat again, if necessary, to insure the soup is hot.

6. Ladle the soup into bowls, top each serving with the grilled shrimp, and garnish with parsley. Serve at once.

OYSTER, LEEK, AND SCALLION SOUP

Serves 6

Fresh oysters are readily available in most regions of the country. Keep them on ice in the refrigerator until you are ready to use them. You can buy the oysters in the shell and shuck them yourself with a sturdy knife, or, if pressed for time, ask the fishmonger to shuck them and reserve the liquor for you. Take care not to overcook the oysters. When their edges begin to curl, they are ready to eat.

Serve this as a soup first course or a light, refreshing main course on a cool summer evening when you're in the mood for a taste of the ocean.

18 small oysters in shells, well scrubbed
2 tablespoons unsalted butter
2 leeks, white and pale green parts only, rinsed and finely chopped
4 scallions, trimmed and finely chopped
4 medium carrots, peeled and cut into julienne about 1½ inches long
2 cups dry white wine
2 cups half-and-half
½ cup heavy cream
Salt and freshly ground black pepper
½ cup finely chopped fresh flat-leaf parsley
Lemon slices, for garnish

1. Shuck the oysters over a bowl and reserve their liquor. Strain the liquor through one or two thicknesses of dampened cheesecloth into another bowl. Set both the oysters and liquor aside.

2. In a skillet, melt the butter over medium-high heat and sauté the leeks and scallions for about 3 minutes, until just softened. Set aside.

3. In a small saucepan, cook the carrots in boiling, salted water to cover over medium-high heat for about 2 minutes, until just barely tender. Drain, pat them dry, and set aside.

4. In a large, nonreactive saucepan or stockpot, bring the wine to a boil over medium-high heat. Remove the pan from the heat and slowly stir in the half-and-half and heavy cream. Stir the mixture constantly to prevent curdling. Return the pan to the stovetop and over medium-high heat bring to a slow boil. Cook, uncovered, for about 5 minutes, until slightly thickened. Reduce the heat to medium-low and stir in the reserved oyster liquor. Add the leeks, scallions, and reserved carrots and cook for about 5 minutes until heated through. Season to taste with salt and pepper.

5. Add the parsley and cook gently for about 2 minutes longer until heated through. Add the oysters and cook, stirring briskly, for about 1 minute, until their edges just begin to curl.

6. Ladle the soup into bowls and garnish by floating the lemon slices. Serve immediately.

OVERLOOKED LEEKS

Leeks, the mildest onion, taste slightly of garlic, too. They are integral to both classic French and Mediterranean cooking but for some reason, Americans haven't wholeheartedly embraced them. Their subtle flavor is wonderful in soups, sauces, and stews and they taste great sautéed in olive oil and butter. Fresh leeks are available nearly all year. They are also easy to grow and can be harvested late into the fall, which extends the glory of the garden.

breads, sandwiches & pizza

The discovery of a new dish
does more for the happiness of man
than the discovery of a star.

—BRILLAT-SAVARIN

GRILLED GARLIC-HERB BREAD

Serves 6 to 8

If you have the time, try roasting the garlic before mixing it with the butter and herbs for a deep, mellow flavor. We use whatever herbs look best in the garden or market—any combination will taste fresh. We like our herb butter packed with herbs but you may prefer subtler flavor. We also recommend buying the best bread you can find, preferably with a crispy crust and soft crumb. This is great with just about anything, but we particularly like it with grilled steak or pasta. You can make this in the broiler as well as on the grill.

1 cup (2 sticks) unsalted butter, softened
2 cloves garlic, finely minced
¼ cup chopped mixed fresh herbs, such as marjoram,
  rosemary, tarragon, and thyme
Salt and freshly ground black pepper
1 large French baguette or Italian bread

1. Put the butter in a small bowl and mash it with a fork. Add the garlic and herbs and mix well. Season to taste with salt and pepper. Cover and set aside at room temperature to give the flavors time to blend.

2. Prepare a charcoal or gas grill. Lightly spray the grill rack with vegetable oil spray to prevent sticking. If using charcoal, let the coals burn until medium-hot to hot, so that they are covered with a thin layer of white ash and are glowing deep red.

3. Cut the baguette in half lengthwise. Cut each half crosswise into thirds or quarters, depending on the size of the baguette and the number of servings you want. Lay the bread slices crust side up on the grill and cook for 1 to 2 minutes, until the bread is lightly browned.

4. Remove the bread from the grill. Spread each slice with butter and return to the grill crust side down. Cover the grill and cook for 2 to 3 minutes, until the butter melts and the crust is lightly browned. Serve hot off the grill.

A PUNGENT HARVEST

easy to grow in nearly any climate, a garlic harvest will enhance your cooking for months to come. In the north, plant it in the spring; in the south, sow in the fall. Plant individual cloves, pointed side up, in the garden and then watch the tender greens sprout (snip them for salads). Store the mature heads in a cool, dry place with plenty of ventilation. Depending on the soil and the kind of garlic used for seed, your homegrown crop will be pungent or mild. Either way, sublime.

ROSEMARY FOCACCIA

Serves 6 to 8; makes 1 large or 2 small loaves

The difference between focaccia and pizza is slight. Focaccia has the flavorings baked right into the bread, while pizza dough is plain, with herbs sprinkled on top. Here we have selected typical but oh-so-delicious Italian flavors: fresh rosemary, snipped from the garden or patio pots, and pungent garlic. If you prefer another herb, by all means substitute it, or try a combination such as fresh thyme, marjoram, tarragon, and rosemary. If you are new to making yeast breads, focaccia is a great place to start. Like most yeast doughs, this is a forgiving one and does not require lengthy kneading or dual rises. In fact, the dough is kneaded for only a few minutes, right in the bowl in which it's mixed. Pretty easy!

1½ cups lukewarm water (105° to 110° F)
1 package (¼ ounce) or 1 scant tablespoon active dry yeast
2 cups bread flour
1½ to 2 cups unbleached all-purpose flour
1 tablespoon salt
2 tablespoons olive oil, plus extra for sprinkling
1 to 2 tablespoons chopped fresh rosemary
1 large clove garlic, sliced
Coarse salt

   1. Pour the water into a large, ceramic or glass mixing bowl and sprinkle the yeast over the water. Stir gently.

   2. Add the bread flour and, using a wooden spoon, stir to mix. Add 1½ cups of the all-purpose flour, the salt, and the olive oil, and stir vigorously to mix. The dough should gather together and pull away from the sides of the bowl, but remain sticky and moist. Add more flour, as necessary, for the correct consistency.

   3. Scoop the dough with lightly oiled or floured hands, and knead gently in the bowl for 2 or 3 minutes, until smooth. Rub the dough on all sides with a little olive oil. Cover the bowl with a kitchen towel or plastic wrap, and set aside in a warm place for about 45 minutes to 1 hour until the dough has doubled.

4. Preheat the oven to 400°F. Lightly oil a baking sheet with olive oil (oil 2 sheets if making 2 small loaves).

5. Using your fist, gently punch the dough down in the bowl. Lift it from the bowl and put it on the oiled sheet (if making 2 loaves, divide the dough in half and put half on each sheet). With lightly oiled fingertips, stretch the dough into a round or rectangular shape about ¼ inch thick. The loaf or loaves should be free-form and rustic looking. From time to time, dip your fingers in olive oil to prevent the dough from sticking.

6. Using your fingertips, make indentations randomly in the stretched dough, breaking through the dough to form craters and rips about 1 inch long. Brush the dough with olive oil, letting it pool in some of the indentations. Sprinkle with rosemary, sliced garlic, and coarse salt.

7. Bake the focaccia for 15 to 20 minutes, until lightly browned. Serve while still warm, breaking off pieces for eating at the table.

▲

AN AL FRESCO
PASTA DINNER

scallop seviche

•

*fettuccine with
sautéed cherry tomatoes
and basil*

•

green salad

•

rosemary focaccia

•

fresh berries and cream

•

chianti

SOUR CREAM CORNBREAD

Serves 6 to 8

We like to bake this the old-fashioned way, in a cast-iron skillet. Cast iron is a great heat conductor and allows the bread to cook evenly and efficiently. This rich, dense bread is good served directly from the skillet but don't stand on ceremony when serving. It will disappear quickly.

1½ cups yellow cornmeal, preferably stone ground
2 teaspoons baking powder
1 teaspoon salt
⅔ cup safflower oil
2 large eggs, at room temperature, lightly beaten
1 container (8 ounces) sour cream
1 can (16 ounces) creamed corn
2 tablespoons minced onion
2 tablespoons finely chopped red pepper
2 ounces sharp Cheddar cheese, grated (about ½ cup)
2 ounces Monterey Jack cheese, grated (about ½ cup)

1. Preheat the oven to 350°F. Oil a 9-inch overproof skillet or a heavyweight 9-by-11-inch baking pan.

2. In a bowl, whisk together the cornmeal, baking powder, and salt.

3. In a medium bowl, stir together the oil, eggs, sour cream, and creamed corn. Stir in the onion and pepper. Scrape this mixture into the cornmeal mixture and stir with a wooden spoon just until blended.

4. Toss the cheeses together in a small bowl.

5. Pour half the batter into the skillet. Scatter the cheeses over the top, mixing them well as you do so. Pour the remaining batter over the cheese, and lightly smooth the top so that it covers the cheese.

6. Bake for about 45 minutes, until the edges of the cornbread begin to brown, the top is set, and a toothpick inserted in the center comes out clean. Let cool in the skillet on a wire rack for at least 30 minutes. Cut into wedges, and serve directly from the skillet.

SOFT-SHELL CRAB SANDWICHES

Serves 6

In the spring and early summer, when soft-shell crabs are at their best, these sandwiches are a luxurious change from the norm. We grill the crabs, but they are also delicious pan-fried. Encase them in soft, fresh rolls, and if you have extra sauce, pass separately. Soft-shell crabs should be alive when you buy them. Ask the fishmonger to clean them for you. When you get them home, refrigerate immediately and cook within a few hours and certainly on the day you purchase them.

SAUCE:

1½ cups mayonnaise
2 tablespoons chopped roasted red bell pepper
  (for how to roast peppers, see page 94)
1 tablespoon chopped sweet gherkin pickle
1 tablespoon chopped shallot
1½ tablespoons chopped fresh thyme
Juice of ½ lemon, or to taste
Salt and freshly ground black pepper

3 tablespoons olive oil
2 tablespoons unsalted butter, melted
1 teaspoon crushed garlic

SANDWICHES:

12 medium soft-shell crabs, cleaned
6 soft potato or kaiser rolls or hamburger buns, split and lightly toasted
Boston or Bibb lettuce
Sliced tomatoes (optional)

  1. To make the sauce: In a small bowl, stir together the mayonnaise, roasted pepper, pickle, shallot, and thyme. Add lemon juice and then season to taste with salt and pepper. Cover and refrigerate until needed.
  2. In a small bowl, mix together the olive oil, butter, and garlic.

3. Prepare a charcoal or gas grill or preheat the broiler. Spray the grill rack with vegetable oil spray to prevent sticking. The coals should be moderately hot, and if charcoal, covered with a substantial coating of white ash and glowing red.

4. To make the sandwiches: Brush the crabs with the butter and oil mixture. When the broiler or the grill is hot, grill the crabs for 4 to 6 minutes, turning once and brushing a few times with melted butter, until they turn dark reddish-brown and the skin begins to get crispy. (Unlike most crabs, these won't turn bright red when done.) Alternatively, sprinkle the crabs with a light coating of flour and cook them in the butter and oil mixture in a large skillet over medium-high heat, turning once or twice, until cooked through, 5 to 7 minutes.

5. Spread some of the sauce on both halves of each roll. Top the bottom with lettuce and tomato, if desired, and then with 2 crabs. Cover with the top portion of the roll and serve immediately.

▲

A SEAFOOD LUNCH
FOR FRIENDS

*oyster, leek, and
scallion soup*

•

*soft-shell
crab sandwiches*

•

*celery root and
cabbage slaw*

•

laura's lemon cookies

•

*fresh-squeezed
lemonade*

•

*iced mint and
lemon verbena tea*

GRILLED CHICKEN AND BASIL MAYONNAISE SANDWICHES

Serves 6

Chicken salad is a mainstay of summer cooking and entertaining. For this recipe you can grill the chicken early in the day, when it's cool, and then serve it later in a salad without losing that grilled goodness. We grill the lemon-marinated chicken until the skin is nicely charred and crisp, then toss it (sometimes with the skin) with a pesto-inspired mayonnaise infused with fresh basil, parsley, garlic, and pine nuts. This salad is great mounded on kaiser or Portuguese rolls fresh from the bakery and topped with radicchio leaves. Serve it with fresh lemonade and enjoy an easy, informal lunch in the garden.

3 whole chicken breasts (about 3 pounds), split
½ cup plus 2 tablespoons fresh lemon juice (about 3 lemons)
Salt and freshly ground black pepper
1½ cups olive oil
2 cups fresh basil leaves, rinsed and patted dry
1 cup chopped fresh flat-leaf parsley
3 tablespoons pine nuts
2 cloves garlic
3 tablespoons mayonnaise
6 kaiser or Portuguese rolls, split
Radicchio leaves

1. Place the chicken in a large glass or ceramic baking dish. Put ½ cup of the lemon juice into a small bowl and season with salt and pepper to taste. Slowly whisk in ¼ cup of the olive oil, and when emulsified, pour over the chicken. Cover and refrigerate for at least 4 hours or overnight, turning occasionally.

2. Prepare a charcoal or gas grill or preheat the broiler. Lightly spray the grill rack with vegetable oil spray to prevent sticking. The coals should be moderately hot to hot, and if charcoal, covered with a thin coating of white ash and glowing deep red.

3. Remove the chicken from the marinade, letting most of it drip back into the dish. Grill or broil the chicken about 6 to 8 inches from the heat for 15 minutes, skin side up. Turn and grill skin side down for about 15 minutes. Turn again and grill for 10 to 15 minutes longer, until the skin is browned and crisp and the juices run clear when the thickest part of the meat is pricked with a fork. An instant-read thermometer inserted into the thickest part of the meat should register 170°F. Baste often with the marinde during the first 20 minutes of grilling.

4. Let the chicken cool. When cool enough to handle, remove the meat from the bones and tear it into pieces about 1½ inches long. Put the meat in a large bowl.

5. Put the basil, parsley, pine nuts, and garlic in the bowl of a food processor fitted with a metal blade and pulse 4 or 5 times. With the machine running, gradually add the remaining ¼ cup of olive oil and process until it is well incorporated. Add the remaining 2 tablespoons of lemon juice and season with salt and pepper to tatse. Scrape the mixture into a bowl and add the mayonnaise, stirring until well mixed. Taste and adjust the seasonings, if necessary.

6. Spoon the basil mayonnaise over the chicken and toss well.

7. Scoop equal portions of the chicken salad on the bottom halves of the rolls and top with radicchio leaves. Place the tops of the rolls over the lettuce and slice the sandwiches in half, if desired.

BEAUTIFUL BASIL

a handful of fresh basil smells like summer, which is one reason it is one of the most popular annuals in the herb garden. It's unbeatable when mixed with fresh mozzarella cheese and tomatoes or tossed into soups or green salads. Basil is the base for traditional pesto, a heavenly blending of basil, garlic, olive oil, pine nuts, and the best Parmesan cheese that is available. Not all basil is the bright green, sweet kind. Other types include anise and cinnamon basil, with hints of those flavors. And pretty opal basil has small, dark, pointy leaves.

GRILLED HAMBURGERS WITH RED ONION SAUCE

Serves 6

Nothing beats grilled hamburgers in the summertime. We make these with a mixture of sirloin and chuck, the former for the flavor, the latter for the moisture contained in the fat. If you don't use chuck, the hamburgers will be dry. We learned this trick from our friends the Lobels, New York butchers with years of experience. These big juicy hamburgers are heavenly when topped with creamy Red Onion Sauce. Decadent, and worth the effort!

1 pound lean ground sirloin
1 pound ground chuck
Salt and freshly ground black pepper
6 hamburger rolls, split
Red Onion Sauce (recipe follows)

▲

4TH OF JULY
BARBECUE

jersey tomato salsa
•
corn chips
•
*grilled hamburgers
with red onion sauce*
•
*grilled corn with
cilantro-cumin butter*
•
herbed potato salad
•
sparkling limeade
•
beer

1. Prepare a charcoal or gas grill or preheat the broiler. Lightly spray the grill rack with vegetable oil spray to prevent sticking. The coals should be moderately-hot to hot, and if charcoal, covered with a thin coating of white ash and glowing deep red.

2. Meanwhile, in a large bowl, mix together the sirloin and chuck and season to taste with salt and pepper. Divide into 6 equal portions and shape into hamburger patties.

3. Grill the hamburgers for about 5 minutes, turn them over, and grill for an additional 4 to 5 minutes for medium to well done burgers. An instant-read thermometer inserted in the middle of a burger should register 150°F.

4. To serve, place the hamburgers on the rolls and spoon some of the Red Onion Sauce over each one. Serve at once.

RED ONION SAUCE

Makes about 2 cups

This delectable sauce is great not only with grilled burgers, but also with grilled pork tenderloin, lamb chops, and vegetables.

4 large red onions, cut into ¼-inch dice
3 cups chicken stock, preferably homemade
½ cup dry sherry
2 tablespoons balsamic vinegar
3 teaspoons sugar
Salt and freshly ground black pepper
¼ cup crème fraîche, low-fat sour cream, or plain yogurt

1. In a saucepan, mix together the onions, stock, sherry, vinegar, and sugar. Bring to a boil over high heat. Reduce the heat and simmer, uncovered, for 40 to 45 minutes, stirring occasionally, until most of the liquid evaporates. Season to taste with salt and pepper.

2. Stir in the crème fraîche and cook over very low heat for about 10 minutes longer, until the flavors blend. Serve warm or at room temperature. Covered and refrigerated, the sauce will keep for up to a week.

GRILLED LAMB BURGERS
WITH COOL CUCUMBER SAUCE

Serves 6

If you've never tried lamb burgers, you are in for a real treat. Lamb, salty black olives, and fresh mint are a natural combination. The burgers are especially good when grilled over a charcoal or gas fire, but you can also broil them indoors. Vary the amount of olives—your preference. Because they are so salty, we don't suggest salting the meat any further. We serve these with a sour cream cucumber sauce flavored with fresh mint, which tastes cool and fresh on these juicy burgers.

COOL CUCUMBER SAUCE:
1 medium cucumber
Salt for sprinkling
1 cup sour cream
1 tablespoon chopped fresh mint leaves
Freshly squeezed lemon juice
Freshly ground white pepper

LAMB BURGERS:
1 tablespoon olive oil
1 medium onion, diced
1 clove garlic, finely chopped
2 pounds ground lamb
3 tablespoons chopped kalamata olives
3 tablespoons chopped fresh flat-leaf parsley
1½ tablespoons chopped fresh mint leaves
Freshly ground black pepper
6 hamburger buns, split

1. To make the sauce: Peel the cucumber and slice it into ¼-inch-thick disks. Transfer to a colander, sprinkle very lightly with salt, and drain for at least 30 to 40 minutes. Spread a layer of paper towels on the work surface and turn the cucumber slices out onto the paper towel in a single layer. Pat dry and chop into ½-inch dice.

2. In a small bowl, combine the diced cucumber, sour cream, and mint leaves and stir gently to mix. Season to taste with lemon juice, salt, and pepper. Cover and set aside at room temperature while preparing the burgers. Do not refrigerate; the sauce may separate.

3. To make the burgers: Heat the olive oil in a large skillet over medium heat. Add the onion and cook, stirring, for 2 to 3 minutes, until just softened. Add the garlic and cook, stirring, for 2 to 3 minutes longer, until the onion is quite soft and the garlic is fragrant but not charred. Set aside to cool.

4. In a large bowl, knead the lamb with your fingers. Add the cooled onion and garlic, the olives, parsley, and mint leaves. Mix well with your hands. Season to taste with pepper.

5. Prepare a charcoal or gas grill. Lightly spray the grill rack with vegetable oil spray to prevent sticking. If using charcoal, let the coals burn until medium-hot to hot, so that they are covered with a thin layer of white ash and are glowing deep red.

6. Meanwhile, form the meat into 6 patties, each about ½ to ¾ inch thick, and refrigerate.

7. Just before grilling, take the burgers from the refrigerator. Grill for about 6 minutes. Turn and grill for 6 or 7 minutes longer, until medium-well done.

8. During the last 2 or 3 minutes of grilling, lay the buns, cut sides down, around the edge of the grill rack and grill until lightly toasted. Serve each burger inside a bun, topped with the cucumber sauce.

SELECTING A BACKYARD GRILL

there are no absolutes when it comes to choosing a grill. For charcoal grilling, we prefer round kettle grills with domed lids that can be removed. When the lid is removed, these grills act like braziers. When it is in place, the dome evenly deflects heat. Gas grills may be fitted with "extras" such as gas burners and rotisseries and some hook up to the main gas line in the house. Others are simpler, with just two or three burners and removable grill racks. These rely on cans of inexpensive propane.

GRILLED LATE-HARVEST PIZZA

Serves 6

Grilling pizza is a freewheeling, communal activity, best designed for people who don't mind sharing the pizzas as they come hot off the grill rather than waiting for their own serving. Everyone can help put the toppings on—or if you prefer, you can man the grill and top the pizzas yourself, while everyone else waits, happily sipping a glass of wine.

This pizza dough is easy to work with and can be used to make oven-baked pizzas as well as grilled ones. Handle the pizzas with care when you first lay them on the grill, and then again when turning them to add the topping. With practice, you will find it easiest to arrange the toppings on the pizzas right on the edge of the grill and then push them back to the hot part of the fire.

Our friend and colleague Deborah Callen, who tested many of the recipes for this book, developed this one for us. It takes advantage of the fresh vegetables and herbs that are so flavorful at the end of the summer, when the gardens are bursting. You can make grilled pizzas any time of year by varying the vegetables and toppings. Try them crowned with sliced tomatoes, fresh mozzarella cheese, and roughly chopped basil or with thinly sliced squash, thyme, garlic, and shredded Monterey Jack cheese. Let your taste be your guide.

DOUGH:

⅓ cup warm water (105° to 110°F)

1 tablespoon honey

1 package (¼ ounce) or 1 scant tablespoon active dry yeast

2 cups bread flour

1¼ cups unbleached all-purpose flour

2 teaspoons salt

2 tablespoons minced fresh rosemary

5 tablespoons extra-virgin olive oil

continued

TOPPINGS:

2 medium eggplants (2¼ to 2½ pounds total weight), peeled and sliced
  into ½-inch-thick slices (12 to 15 slices per eggplant)
Coarse salt for sprinkling
½ cup extra-virgin olive oil
4 cloves garlic, crushed
3 red bell peppers, stemmed, seeded, and halved
1 pound plum or other tomatoes, seeded and cut into thin strips
1 medium sweet white onion, cut into very thin slices
2 tablespoons sherry vinegar
Salt and freshly ground black pepper
1 pound soft, fresh goat cheese
8 ounces feta cheese, crumbled
1 cup freshly grated Parmesan cheese
2 tablespoons minced fresh oregano
1 tablespoon minced fresh mint
2 teaspoons grated lemon zest
1 teaspoon freshly ground black pepper

½ cup finely chopped fresh flat-leaf parsley, for garnish
Red pepper flakes, for garnish

1. To make the dough: Stir together the water and honey in a small bowl or glass measuring cup. Sprinkle with yeast and set aside.

2. In a large bowl, combine the flours, salt, and rosemary and whisk 8 or 9 times, until blended.

3. Stir 3 tablespoons of the olive oil into the yeast. Add to the flour and stir with a wooden spoon until the dough holds together.

4. Turn the dough out onto a lightly floured work surface and gently knead for 3 to 5 minutes, or until it's smooth and elastic. Divide into 6 equal portions, each about 5 ounces, Flatten into small disks.

5. Pour the remaining 2 tablespoons of oil onto a baking sheet and spread it out over a large portion of the sheet. Put the disks of dough on the baking sheet, and turn them several times to coat lightly with the oil.

Add a little more oil, if necessary. Arrange the disks on the baking sheet and loosely cover the entire sheet with plastic wrap. Set aside in a warm place for about 30 minutes until doubled in bulk.

6. To prepare the topping: Put the eggplant slices in a large colander, sprinkling each layer generously with coarse salt. Set aside over a plate or sink for about 30 minutes to drain. Remove the slices from the colander and pat dry with paper towels, removing as much salt as possible.

7. In a small bowl, stir together ¼ cup of the olive oil and the garlic. Lay the eggplant slices and the pepper halves on baking sheets and brush with the garlic oil. Set aside.

8. In a small, glass or ceramic bowl, toss together the tomatoes and onion. Add the remaining ¼ cup of olive oil and the vinegar. Toss gently and season to taste with salt and pepper.

9. In another bowl, stir together the goat cheese, feta, Parmesan, oregano, mint, lemon zest, and pepper.

10. Prepare a charcoal or gas grill. Spray the grill rack with vegetable oil spray to prevent sticking. If using charcoal, let the coals burn until they are covered with a thin layer of white ash and glowing deep red.

11. Rub oil on a clean, dry baking sheet and transfer 2 of the disks to it. Using the heel of your hand, flatten them into rounds ranging from 9 to 12 inches in diameter. They don't have to be perfectly shaped. Thinner (and larger) pizzas will have crispier crusts. Carefully lift the rounds from the baking sheet and lay them on the hot grill. Close the grill and cook for 1 to 2 minutes, until the bottoms of the crusts have grill marks. Using tongs, lay the crusts, grilled side up, on the baking sheet.

12. Spoon a heaping ¼ cup of the cheese mixture on each crust and spread it over the surface, leaving a narrow border. Lay 4 slices of eggplant and several strips of pepper on each pizza. Using a slotted spoon, scatter a heaping spoonful of the tomato salad over the eggplant. With a broad spatula and your fingers, carefully transfer the pizzas back to the grill. Cover and cook for 3 to 4 minutes, or until the vegetables are heated through and the cheese is hot.

13. Sprinkle each pizza with parsley and pepper flakes and serve at once. Repeat with the remaining disks of dough, cheese, and vegetables.

main courses

Strange to see how a good dinner and feasting reconciles everybody.

—SAMUEL PEPYS

GRILLED CHICKEN BREASTS WITH CHOPPED AVOCADO SALAD

Serves 6

Chicken is tricky on the grill. The white meat cooks too fast; the dark meat takes forever. We like to separate the two and cook only chicken breasts, as here, or only legs and thighs. For the best success, begin grilling the chicken skin-side down and then turn it several times with tongs. A fork will pierce the skin and the meat will lose valuable juices. For this, the chicken is first marinated in a citrusy bath, and is served with an easy avocado salad with Southwestern flair.

CHICKEN:

Juice of 2 limes (about ½ cup)
¼ cup orange juice, preferably fresh
1 tablespoon olive oil
Salt and freshly ground black pepper
3 whole chicken breasts (about 3 pounds), split

SALAD:

3 ripe avocados, peeled, pitted, and cut into small dice
2 medium tomatoes, finely diced
1 small red onion, finely diced
¼ cup chopped cilantro
¼ cup chopped flat-leaf parsley
Juice of 1 lime (about ¼ cup)
2 tablespoons sour cream
1 teaspoon ground cumin
Salt and freshly ground black pepper
3 cups mixed salad greens
Parsley sprigs, for garnish

AVOCADOS

avocados may come under the heading of "indulgence"—but as the essential ingredient in guacamole, how could it get any better? Their rich, buttery flesh adds unmistakable flavor and texture to salads and sandwiches, and the fruit itself is outstanding when halved, pit removed, and filled with shrimp, crabmeat, or chicken salad. They are available most of the year, but most noticeably in winter and summer. Small, dark, and dimpled Haas avocados are preferred by most, although when fresh, larger, smooth, pale green Fuerte are great. Ripe fruit gives to gentle pressure when pressed.

continued

1. To prepare the chicken: In a bowl, whisk together the lime juice, orange juice, and olive oil. Season to taste with salt and pepper. Arrange the chicken breasts in a shallow, glass or ceramic dish and pour the marinade over them. Turn several times to coat. Cover and refrigerate for at least 2 hours or overnight. Turn occasionally during soaking.

2. Prepare a charcoal or gas grill. Lightly spray the grill rack with vegetable oil spray to prevent sticking. Let the coals burn until medium-hot to hot so that they are covered with a thin layer of white ash and are glowing deep red.

3. Lift the chicken from the marinade, letting it drip back into the dish. Put the chicken on the grill, skin side facing the heat, and grill or broil about 6 to 8 inches from the heat for 30 to 40 minutes, turning several times with tongs, until nicely browned and the juices run clear when pricked with a fork. An instant-read thermometer inserted into the thickest part of the meat should register 170°F. Baste the chicken with the marinade during the first 20 minutes of grilling.

4. To make the salad: Put the avocados, tomatoes, onion, cilantro, and parsley in a mixing bowl. Add the lime juice, sour cream, cumin, and salt and pepper to taste and gently stir with a fork until mixed. Arrange the salad greens on each plate. Put a chicken breast on top of the greens and spoon the avocado salad next to it. Garnish with parsley sprigs and serve at once.

▲

SANTA FE SUPPER

*spicy yellow tomato
gazpacho*
•
*grilled chicken breasts
with chopped
avocado salad*
•
sour cream corn bread
•
green salad
•
*fresh peaches
and raspberries*
•
pinot noir

GRILLED CORNISH GAME HENS WITH MINT SAUCE

Serves 6

Little cornish game hens are a treat cooked on the grill. Everyone gets one whole bird, although if there are light eaters or children in the group, you could split one bird between two. This simple marinade takes advantage of the fresh mint that grows so easily in so many gardens. It's also delicious on chicken.

HENS:

¼ cup olive oil

¼ cup white wine vinegar

2 tablespoons chopped fresh mint

2 teaspoons sugar

Six 1- to 1¼-pound Cornish game hens

Salt and freshly ground black pepper

6 sprigs fresh mint

2 tart, firm apples, peeled, cored, and chopped

SAUCE:

½ cup mint jelly

3 tablespoons cider vinegar

3 tablespoons water

1 tablespoon chopped fresh mint leaves

1 tart, firm apple, peeled, cored, and finely chopped

1 shallot, finely chopped

Salt and freshly ground black pepper

   1. To prepare the hens: In a small bowl, combine the olive oil, vinegar, mint, and sugar. Stir to dissolve the sugar.

   2. Generously season the hens with salt and pepper and lay them in a shallow, glass or ceramic dish. Pour the marinade over the hens and rub

continued

them with the liquid, taking care to rub inside the cavities as well as outside the birds. Insert a sprig of mint and a little chopped apple inside each cavity. Using kitchen twine, truss the hens by tying the legs together.

3. Prepare a charcoal or gas grill. Lightly spray the grill rack with vegetable oil cooking spray. Let the coals heat until moderately hot, covered with a substantial layer of white ash and glowing red.

4. Lift the hens from the marinade, letting any excess drip back in the pan. Discard the marinade. Grill the hens, breast side down, for about 15 minutes. Turn and grill for 25 to 30 minutes longer or until the juices run clear when the thickest part of the breast meat is pricked with a fork or sharp knife and an instant-read thermometer registers 180°F. The skin should be browned and crisp. Let the hens rest for about 5 minutes before serving.

5. To make the sauce: In a small saucepan, mix together all the ingredients except salt and pepper. Heat over medium-low heat, stirring until the jelly melts. Season to taste with salt and pepper. Pass on the side.

SPICY SOUTHWESTERN-STYLE GRILLED FLANK STEAK

Serves 6

Flank steak is a great choice for outdoor grilling, although you can broil it successfully, too. It's a lean, flat, boneless cut of meat with slender fibers running lengthwise through it. Because it has little marbling, it's tougher than sirloin, porterhouse, or filet mignon and thus benefits from marinating. It also should be sliced on the diagonal, through the fibers, once it's cooked. Flank steak is sometimes labeled London broil. (London broil is not a cut but a term for any relatively thin cut of meat that is grilled or broiled and then sliced on the diagonal into strips. It most often is flank steak or round steak.)

The spicy marinade gives the meat a slightly Southwestern flavor. To accentuate the flavor, brush the marinade on the meat during grilling, but as with all marinades, stop using it after the first minutes of grilling because the marinade must have time to cook so that any bacteria from the raw meat are rendered harmless. Serve this with grilled red and yellow peppers, rice, and salsa.

½ cup safflower or canola oil
½ cup fresh lime juice (4 to 5 limes)
2 tablespoons cider vinegar
4 scallions, white and green parts, sliced
2 jalapeños, seeded and coarsely chopped
1 clove garlic, chopped
2 tablespoons chopped cilantro
1 tablespoon chili powder
1 teaspoon cumin
3 pounds flank steak
Chopped cilantro, for garnish (optional)

1. In a bowl, stir together the oil, lime juice, and vinegar. Add the scallions, jalapeños, garlic, cilantro, chili powder, and cumin. Mix well.

2. Lay the flank steak in a shallow, glass or ceramic dish. Pour the marinade over the meat, spreading it over the surface of the meat and turning the steak to coat on both sides. Cover and refrigerate for at least 1 hour or overnight. About 20 minutes before grilling, remove the meat from the refrigerator and let it sit at room temperature.

3. Prepare a charcoal or gas grill. First spray the grill rack with vegetable oil spray to prevent sticking. The coals should be moderately-hot to hot, and if charcoal, covered with a thin coating of white ash and glowing deep red.

4. Lift the steak from the dish, letting the marinade drip back into it. Grill the steak for 6 to 7 minutes, brushing several times with the marinade during the first 5 minutes of grilling. (The oil in the marinade may cause flare-ups. Have a spray bottle filled with water on hand to extinguish them.) Turn the steak and grill for 6 to 7 minutes longer until medium rare, or until it reaches the desired degree of doneness. The meat is medium rare when the thermometer registers 140° to 145°F.

5. Let the steak rest at room temperature for about 5 minutes. Slice on the diagonal into thin strips and serve, garnished with cilantro, if desired.

▲

STEAK
ON THE GRILL

*spicy southwestern-style
grilled flank steak*

•

*grilled red and
yellow peppers*

•

tomato-mango salsa

•

rice

•

grilled garlic-herb bread

•

*warm crêpes with
summer blueberries
and peaches*

•

merlot

GRILLED VEAL CHOPS
WITH WILD MUSHROOM SAUCE

Serves 6

When reconstituted, woodsy "wild mushrooms" are as soft and delicious as they are when fresh—maybe even better. The soaking liquid, whether it's wine, broth, or water, is rich and delicious too, but has to be strained before it's used. Here, they mingle with fresh white mushrooms in a light sauce that is excellent with grilled veal chops but would be just as good with steak or burgers. Buy thick veal chops; they are worth every penny when perfectly grilled.

1½ ounces assorted dried wild mushrooms
1 cup Madeira wine
4 tablespoons unsalted butter
6 garlic cloves, finely minced
2 shallots, peeled and chopped
3 cups stemmed and thinly sliced white mushrooms
Salt and freshly ground black pepper
2 tablespoons chopped fresh flat-leaf parsley
1 tablespoon fresh lemon juice
Six 12-ounce rib or loin veal chops, about 1½ inches thick
Olive oil for brushing

   1. Using a small strainer, rinse the dried mushrooms under cold running water. Drain and transfer to a small bowl. Add the wine and let the mushrooms soak for at least 1 hour or until softened.

   2. Melt 2 tablespoons of the butter in a large skillet over medium-high heat. Add the garlic and shallots and cook for about 5 minutes until golden. Add the sliced fresh mushrooms and cook, stirring, over high heat for about 5 minutes until they begin to release their juices and soften. Set aside.

   3. Using a slotted spoon, remove the dried mushrooms from the bowl. Transfer to a cutting board and chop coarsely.

4. Add the remaining 2 tablespoons butter to the skillet and cook over medium-high heat until the butter melts. Add the chopped dried mushrooms and season to taste with salt and pepper. Cook over low heat for about 10 minutes, stirring occasionally, until the mixture is well blended and fragrant.

5. Strain the soaking liquid from the mushrooms through a fine sieve. Add to the skillet, reduce the heat to low, and cook for about 5 minutes until heated through. Add the parsley and lemon juice, taste, and adjust the seasonings, if necessary. The sauce can be made up to 2 hours ahead of time. Reheat over low heat just before serving.

6. Prepare a charcoal or gas grill. Lightly spray the grill rack with vegetable oil cooking spray. Let the coals heat until moderately hot to hot so that they are covered with a light coating of white ash and glow deep red.

7. Brush the veal chops with olive oil and sprinkle generously with salt and pepper. Grill for 8 to 10 minutes per side for medium rare, and a few minutes longer for better done. An instant-read thermometer inserted in the thickest part of the meat should read 140°F for medium rare and 150°F for medium.

8. Serve with generous portions of the warm mushroom sauce spooned over each chop.

WILD MUSHROOMS
Unless you know what you are doing, buy "wild mushrooms"; don't forage for them in the woods. Many grocers and farmers' markets sell a wide variety, from common white to more exotic morels, cepes, cloud ear, and oyster. Shiitake and cremini are two of the most common wild mushrooms. Giant portobello mushrooms are simply mature cremini. Depending on the type, look for smooth caps and unbroken gills. Their earthiness and deep flavor make mushrooms a great favorite, especially paired with autumn harvest vegetables.

GRILLED PORK-AND-PINEAPPLE KABOBS WITH SCALLIONS

Serves 6

While few gardens produce fresh pineapples, the duo of pork and pineapples is so good we could not resist these simple, grilled kabobs. Here, we suggest serving them alongside grilled scallions, although grilled red or yellow peppers would be delicious, too. We like our pineapple nicely charred, but you may want to load a few skewers with meat and others with pineapple so that you can grill the pineapple for only eight to 10 minutes.

1½ cups pineapple juice
Juice of 3 limes
3 tablespoons olive oil
3 tablespoons brown sugar
3 to 4 scallions, roughly chopped
2½ pounds trimmed boned pork loin or butt, cut into 1½-inch cubes
One 3¾- to 4¼-pound fresh pineapple
12 large scallions, trimmed
Olive oil for brushing

1. In a large, glass or ceramic bowl, mix together the pineapple juice, lime juice, olive oil, and brown sugar. Add the scallions and stir to mix. Add the pork, toss to coat, cover, and refrigerate for at least 4 and up to 12 hours, stirring several times during soaking.

2. Trim the leaves off the pineapple. Hold the pineapple upright on a cutting board and slice the skin off the fruit. Slice the peeled fruit in half and cut out the core. Cut the fruit into 1½- to 2-inch chunks. You will have about 4 cups of cubes, or about 18 cubes.

3. Prepare a charcoal or gas grill. First spray the grill rack with vegetable oil spray to prevent sticking. The coals should be moderately hot, and if charcoal, covered with a thin coating of gray ash and glowing red.

continued

4. Thread the pork and pineapple chunks on six 12-inch skewers, beginning and ending with chunks of pork. Each skewer should have approximately 6 cubes of meat and 3 cubes of pineapple. Discard the marinade.

5. Grill for 12 to 15 minutes, turning several times, or until the meat reaches the desired degree of doneness and the pineapple is lightly charred. To check for doneness, insert an instant-read thermometer into a thick piece of meat. The thermometer should register 155°F or slightly higher.

6. Meanwhile, lay the scallions on the outer edges of the grill. Brush them lightly with olive oil and grill for about 5 minutes, turning with tongs until charred.

7. Remove the pork and pineapple from the skewers and serve with the scallions.

GRILLED LAMB CHOPS WITH MINTED MANGO CHUTNEY

Serves 6

A fresh chutney made from juicy tropical fruits and fresh mint offsets the irresistible flavor of lamb chops—which are a rare treat. Buy loin or rib chops, not shoulder chops which may cost less but won't be as tender and flavorful.

CHUTNEY:

2 cups diced mango (2 mangos)
½ cup diced kiwi (2 kiwi)
¼ cup chopped red onions
1 jalapeño, seeded and diced
2 tablespoons fresh lime juice
3 tablespoons finely chopped fresh mint
1 teaspoon light brown sugar or honey

CHOPS:

12 loin or rib lamb chops, each about 2 inches thick
Freshly ground black pepper

1. To make the chutney: Combine the mango, kiwi, onions, jalapeño, lime juice, mint, and sugar. Stir gently and set aside while grilling the chops. Or cover and refrigerate for up to 3 hours. Let the chutney come to cool room temperature before serving.

2. To grill the chops: Generously season the lamb chops with pepper.

3. Prepare a charcoal or gas grill. Lightly spray the grill rack with vegetable oil spray. Let the coals heat until moderately-hot to hot so that they are covered with a light coating of white ash and glow deep red.

4. Grill the lamb chops for 5 to 6 minutes on each side until medium rare, or cooked to desired degree of doneness or an instant-read thermometer registers 140°F for rare, 150°F for medium, or 160°F for well-done meat. Season with a little more pepper just before serving, if desired. Pass the chutney on the side.

FRESH MINT

As a hardy perennial, mint happily grows (and grows and grows!) in almost all climates. Without surveillance, it will overtake the herb garden. The varieties are endless, and all share the distinctive mint flavor. Peppermint and spearmint are the two classic culinary mints, with spearmint tasting mintier and peppermint tasting spicier. More than 500 mints have been hybridized, such as apple mint, cinnamon mint, and lemon mint, which have subtle undertones of those flavors. Mint leaves are small and pointed, in varying shades of green.

MIXED GRILL OF SAUSAGES WITH TARRAGON-MUSTARD SAUCE

Serves 6

A favorite menu of ours includes a grill of mixed sausages. Since there are so many varieties of good sausage available in specialty markets and butcher shops these days, you can pick and choose your favorites. The sausages may be hot, spicy, mild, or sweet. Try to serve two or three different kinds to each guest. A good rule of thumb is to serve eight ounces per person. This mixed grill is delicious with Warm Lentils and Sautéed Spinach (page 117).

TARRGON-MUSTARD SAUCE:
⅓ cup Dijon Mustard
2 tablespoons rice wine vinegar
2 tablespoons chopped fresh tarragon leaves
Freshly ground black pepper

GRILLED SAUSAGES:
2½ pounds mixed sausages, in coils

1. To make the Tarragon-Mustard Sauce: In a bowl, stir together the mustard, vinegar, tarragon, and pepper.

2. Prepare a gas or charcoal grill. Lightly spray the grill rack with vegetable oil spray. Let the coals heat until moderately-hot to hot so that they are covered with a light coating of white ash and glow deep red.

3. To make the Grilled Sausages: Pierce each sausage with 2 skewers at right angles to hold shape and facilitate turning.

4. Grill the sausages for 10 to 15 minutes, turning once, until cooked through and lightly charred.

5. Cut the sausages into large pieces and serve immediately with the Tarragon-Mustard Sauce.

▲

EARLY AUTUMN LUNCH IN THE GARDEN

red lettuce salad

•

mixed grill of sausages with tarragon-mustard sauce

•

warm lentils and sautéed spinach

•

buffalo bay apple crisp

•

cabernet sauvignon

ROASTED HALIBUT
WITH PARSLEY-LEMON SAUCE

Serves 6

This is a quick and delicious way to prepare halibut, a wonderful fish
that is readily available. The fish is simply sautéed on both sides, then
roasted in the oven and topped with a fresh parsley sauce which can be
made up to a day ahead of time.

PARSLEY-LEMON SAUCE:
1 cup finely chopped fresh flat-leaf parsley
1 clove garlic, chopped
Salt and freshly ground pepper
½ cup extra-virgin olive oil
1 tablespoon freshly grated Parmesan cheese
1 teaspoon fresh lemon juice

HALIBUT:
2 teaspoons unsalted butter
2 teaspoons olive oil
Six 8-ounce halibut steaks
Salt and freshly ground black pepper

   1. To make the Parsley-Lemon Sauce: Put the parsley, garlic, and salt
and pepper to taste in a food processor fitted with a metal blade or a
blender. Pulse 4 or 5 times. With the machine running, add the olive oil
in a thin stream until well incorporated and smooth. Scrape the mixture
into a bowl or storage container.

   2. Add the cheese and lemon juice to the parsley mixture and stir
gently. Cover and refrigerate until ready to serve. Remove the sauce
from the refrigerator about 30 minutes before serving. The sauce can be
made up to 1 day ahead of time.

continued

PARSLEY'S DAY

thankfully, we have moved well beyond the days when parsley was considered only a garnish, and a boring one at that! Bright green, flat-leaf parsley, also called Italian parsley, has a lovely grassy flavor that when added to a dish helps the other flavors "pop." It grows nicely in the garden or pot and is also available fresh all year long in the market. Don't confuse it with cilantro, which looks very much like it but tastes totally different. Curly parsley is still reserved mostly for garnish (and it's still boring).

3. To prepare the fish: Preheat the oven to 375°F. Heat the butter and olive oil in a nonstick skillet over medium-high heat until the butter melts. Sear the fish, turning once, until nicely browned on both sides. Season the fish with salt and pepper on both sides.

4. Transfer the fish to a nonstick baking pan and roast for 5 to 7 minutes until cooked through and just beginning to flake when prodded with a fork. Spoon a little of the sauce over each steak and serve at once.

POACHED SALMON SALAD WITH MUSTARD DRESSING

Serves 6

Serving poached salmon in the spring is almost a requirement for the home cook! This recipe takes advantage of another of spring's most elegant crops: asparagus. Cook it only until crisp-tender so that it is not limp when mixed with the salmon.

1 bunch asparagus spears (12 to 14 spears)

SALMON:
1½ quarts water
1 cup dry white wine
2 carrots, coarsely chopped
1 small onion, sliced
10 peppercorns (about ¼ teaspoon)
1 bay leaf
Parsley sprigs
6 skinned salmon steaks, about ¾-inch thick, or skinned salmon fillets (total of about 3 pounds of salmon)

3 tablespoons white wine or Champagne vinegar
1 tablespoon Dijon mustard
½ cup extra-virgin olive oil
2 tablespoons chopped shallot
1 to 2 teaspoons chopped fresh dill
Salt and freshly ground black pepper

2 bunches fresh watercress, for serving
2 cucumbers, thinly sliced, for garnish
Lemon wedges, for garnish

1. To poach the asparagus and salmon: Combine the water, wine, carrots, onion, peppercorns, bay leaf, and parsley sprigs in a large, deep skillet. Bring to a boil over high heat. Reduce the heat to a simmer and add the asparagus spears. Poach for 3 to 4 minutes, or until the asparagus is crisp-tender. Using tongs, lift the asparagus from the poaching liquid and set aside to drain and cool.

2. Add the salmon to the simmering poaching liquid, cover, and poach for about 15 minutes or until the salmon is cooked through. An instant-read thermometer inserted into the meat should register 140°F. Lift the salmon from the poaching liquid and set aside to cool.

3. To make the dressing: Whisk together the vinegar and mustard. Slowly add the olive oil, whisking, until emulsified. Stir in the shallot and dill and season to taste with salt and pepper.

4. Flake or cut the salmon into bite-sized chunks. Chop the asparagus into 1½- to 2-inch lengths. Put the salmon and asparagus in a bowl and toss gently to mix. Spoon the dressing over the salmon.

5. Arrange the watercress on a platter and spoon the salmon salad over it. Garnish with cucumber slices and lemon wedges, and serve.

FISH FRY WITH HERBED TARTAR SAUCE

Serves 6

Fried lemony fish fillets served with a homemade tartar sauce packed with fresh herbs from the garden make a simple and delicious meal. We prefer flounder, but any mild, white-fleshed fish, such as bass or snapper, is delicious.

¾ cup unbleached all-purpose flour, plus more for coating
¼ teaspoon baking soda
Salt and freshly ground black pepper
1 cup milk
1 large egg, lightly beaten
2 tablespoons club soda
2 teaspoons fresh lemon juice
Safflower oil
Twelve 6-ounce flounder fillets, rinsed and patted dry
Herbed Tartar Sauce (recipe follows)

1. In a large, shallow bowl, whisk together the flour, baking soda, and salt and pepper to taste. Stir in the milk, egg, club soda, and lemon juice and set aside for 30 minutes.

2. Spread about a ½ inch of flour in a shallow dish.

3. Heat about 1 inch of oil in a large skillet or 2 medium skillets over high heat.

4. Lay each fillet in the flour and turn to coat. Dip the fillet in the batter and then let the excess drip back into the bowl. Fry the fillets, in batches if necessary, for about 6 minutes, turning once with tongs, until golden brown and cooked through. Drain on paper towels. If working in batches, cover the fish and keep them warm in a low (200°F) oven. Serve immediately with tartar sauce.

HERBED TARTAR SAUCE

Makes about 1¼ cups

This tasty tartar sauce, made with homemade mayonnaise, is very easy to make with a food processor and room-temperature ingredients. The trick is to add the oils in a slow, steady stream; don't get impatient. This way, the ingredients will emulsify into a silken sauce. If you prefer using commercial mayonnaise, please do. And use it, too, if you have any concern regarding the raw egg in the recipe.

1 large egg
1 tablespoon fresh lemon juice
1 teaspoon Dijon mustard
Pinch of salt
Dash of hot pepper sauce, such as Tabasco
¾ cup safflower oil
¼ cup olive oil
2 tablespoons finely diced dill pickle
1 tablespoon small capers, drained
1 tablespoon fresh chives
1 tablespoon fresh tarragon
1 tablespoon chopped fresh flat-leaf parsley
Freshly ground black pepper

   1. In the bowl of a food processor fitted with the metal blade, put the egg, lemon juice, mustard, salt and hot pepper sauce. With the motor running, slowly pour the oils in a steady stream through the feed tube. When thoroughly blended, turn off the machine, scrape down the sides, and taste and adjust the seasonings, if necessary. Scrape into a container, cover, and refrigerate for up to 5 days.

   2. About 1 hour before serving, fold the pickle, capers, chives, tarragon, and parsley into the mayonnaise. Season to taste with pepper. Cover and refrigerate until serving.

▲
FRIDAY NIGHT
FISH FRY

*iced cucumber soup with
yogurt and dill*

•

*fish fry with
herbed tartar sauce*

•

snow pea–orange salad

•

summer berry shortcake

•

vanilla ice cream

•

chardonnay

GRILLED SALADE NIÇOISE WITH FRESH GARDEN VEGETABLES

Serves 6

Inspired by a dish created by our friend Rick Rodgers, this is a surefire winner for a summer supper. You will need lots of grill space for all the vegetables, or you can grill them earlier in the day to serve at room temperature with the just-grilled tuna. Use the finest extra-virgin olive oil.

TUNA:

⅔ cup olive oil
Juice of 1 lemon
¼ cup shredded basil leaves
Freshly ground black pepper
Two 8- to 9-ounce tuna steaks, each about 1 inch thick

SALAD:

1 pound small red or white new potatoes
2 red bell peppers, seeded, trimmed, and cut into 2-inch chunks
¼ cup olive oil
Juice of 1 lemon
1 clove garlic, minced
Salt and freshly ground black pepper
3 beefsteak tomatoes, cored and cut into 1- to 1½-inch-thick slices
1 large red onion, sliced into 1 to 1½-inch-thick slices
12 medium-thick spears asparagus, ends snapped
1 head Boston lettuce or 2 heads Bibb lettuce
½ pound cherry tomatoes, halved, for garnish
½ cup Niçoise olives, for garnish
Extra-virgin olive oil, for drizzling

1. To prepare the tuna: In a shallow glass or ceramic bowl, combine the olive oil, lemon juice, and basil. Season to taste with pepper. Mix

continued

well and then add the tuna steaks, turning them several times to coat. Cover and refrigerate for 1 hour, turning several times.

2. Prepare a charcoal or gas grill. Lightly spray the grill rack with vegetable oil spray. The coals should be hot and covered with gray ash.

3. To prepare the salad: Scrub the potatoes and halve or quarter any that are especially large. They should be the right size to thread on skewers without falling off. Thread the potatoes on metal skewers (threading them on 2 parallel skewers will prevent them from twisting). Lay the skewers on a baking sheet.

4. Thread the pepper chunks on skewers and lay them on the baking sheet next to the potatoes.

5. In a glass or ceramic bowl, combine the olive oil, lemon juice, and garlic, and season to taste with salt and pepper. Generously brush the potatoes and peppers with the olive oil mixture and set aside.

6. Lay the tomatoes, onion slices, and asparagus spears on a baking sheet or similar pan and brush with the olive oil mixture.

7. Grill the potatoes and peppers for about 20 minutes, turning the skewers several times, until tender.

8. Meanwhile, lift the tuna steaks from the marinade, let the marinade drip back into the dish, and let the tuna come to cool room temperature. Grill for 6 or 7 minutes, turning it once. Take care not to overcook; when it is just beginning to flake, it is ready.

9. At the same time, lay the tomato and onion slices and asparagus spears on the grill, near the edge. Grill for 6 or 7 minutes, or a little longer, until softened and lightly charred.

10. Spread the lettuce on a serving platter. Slice the tuna and arrange it on the lettuce. Arrange the potatoes and peppers around the tuna, along with the grilled tomatoes and onions. You may want to halve the tomato and onion slices. Lay the asparagus spears over the tuna in a decorative pattern. Garnish the platter with the cherry tomatoes and olives. Drizzle some olive oil over the fish and vegetables. Season to taste with salt and pepper and serve.

Note: If you grill the vegetables ahead of time, refrigerate them once cooled but let them come to room temperature before serving.

FETTUCCINE WITH SAUTÉED CHERRY TOMATOES AND BASIL

Serves 6

Quick, fresh tomato sauce is a summertime pleasure and this one, made with sweet cherry tomatoes, is at one time both rich tasting and light. We like to use fresh pasta whenever possible, but this could be made with dried pasta—cook it according to the package directions.

3 tablespoons olive oil
2 cloves garlic, finely chopped
3 pints red or yellow cherry tomatoes, stemmed and halved
  or quartered, depending on their size
¼ cup white wine
¼ cup chicken broth
Dried red pepper flakes
Salt and freshly ground black pepper
1½ pounds fresh fettuccine
1 cup loosely packed torn fresh basil leaves

   1. In a large frying pan, heat the olive oil over medium heat. Add the garlic and cook, stirring, for 2 to 3 minutes until fragrant but not browned. Add the tomatoes and cook, stirring gently, for 2 to 3 minutes until they just begin to soften.

   2. Add the wine and chicken broth and flavor to taste with pepper flakes, salt, and pepper. Lower the heat to low and cook for 5 to 7 minutes, stirring only occasionally. The tomatoes should not completely lose their shape.

   3. Meanwhile, in a large pot of boiling, salted water, cook the pasta for 2 to 3 minutes or until al dente. Drain and transfer to the frying pan. Remove the pan from the heat, and toss the pasta with the tomatoes. Sprinkle the basil leaves over the hot pasta and toss once or twice to mix just barely. Serve at once.

EDIBLE FLOWERS

most people think of nasturtiums first when searching for edible flowers. These pretty, easy-to-grow annuals, which range from deep yellow to bright orange, add beauty and peppery flavor to salads and cold platters. They can be grown in pots or along the border of vegetable or flower gardens, as long as they are exposed to good sun. Harvest the blooms and, as with pansies, which are also edible, more will grow. Other edible flowers include pansies and violas, roses, lavender, chive blossoms, garlic flowers, and zucchini blossoms.

ROASTED RED PEPPERS STUFFED WITH FRESH CORN AND ZUCCHINI

Serves 4 as a main course; serves 8 as a side dish

While this won't make much of a dent in your bumper crop of zucchini, these vegetable-stuffed red bell peppers make a lovely light meal or side dish. Partially cooking the peppers first is necessary to insure that they are completely cooked when served.

4 large red bell peppers, halved lengthwise, seeded but stems intact
2 teaspoons olive oil
1 medium onion, finely chopped
2 cloves garlic, thinly sliced
2 jalapeños, seeded and minced
1 pound small zucchini, trimmed and diced (about 3 zucchini)
2 cups fresh corn kernels (2 to 3 ears)
¼ cup chopped cilantro
¼ cup chopped flat-leaf parsley
Salt and freshly ground black pepper
2 ounces Monterey Jack cheese, grated (about ½ cup)

1. Preheat the oven to 450°F. Lightly oil a baking sheet and a 9-by-13-inch baking dish.

2. Put the peppers cut side down on the baking sheet and bake for 8 to 10 minutes until just tender. Remove the peppers from the oven and reduce the oven temperature to 375°F. Arrange the peppers, cut side up, in the baking dish.

3. In a large skillet, heat the olive oil over medium heat. Add the onion and cook, stirring occasionally, for 3 to 5 minutes until softened. Add the garlic and jalapeño and cook, stirring, for about 1 minute. Add the zucchini and corn, cover, and cook for about 10 minutes, stirring occasionally, until the vegetables are tender. Stir in the cilantro and parsley and season to taste with salt and pepper.

*grilled portobello
mushroom salad with
herbed goat cheese*

•

*roasted red peppers
stuffed with fresh corn
and zucchini*

•

*haricots verts with
parsley-pecan pesto*

•

peach sorbet

•

laura's lemon cookies

•

*iced mint and
lemon verbena tea*

4. Spoon about ¼ cup of filling into each pepper half. Sprinkle each with cheese. (At this point, the peppers can be allowed to cool to room temperature, covered, and refrigerated for up to 24 hours.)

5. Add about 2 tablespoons of water into the dish, cover with foil, and bake the peppers for about 20 minutes or until heated through. Uncover and bake for about 5 minutes longer until the cheese is soft and melted. Serve immediately.

Variation: For a change of pace, stuff pretty yellow or orange peppers with cooked cous cous tossed with dried currants, scallions, and fresh herbs such as parsley, cilantro, and dill. Chop cooked spinach and toss it into the filling, too, before spooning into the cooked pepper shells. Serve at room temperature or warmed for about 20 minutes in a 350°F. oven.

ZUCCHINI ZEALOTRY

What can you do with all the zucchini choking the garden? This is a common plea among vegetable gardeners, who, come September, tend to pass out zucchini to friends and neighbors like new fathers pass out cigars. Luckily, this most popular member of the summer squash family can be eaten raw, sliced and sautéed, layered in casseroles, pureed for soups, or shredded and baked into quick breads and muffins. Zucchini is best in its season, recently harvested from a local farm or garden. Once you taste it, you'll be glad it's so versatile.

salads & side dishes

She digs in her garden
With a shovel and a spoon,
She weeds her lazy lettuce
By the light of the moon.

—EDNA ST. VINCENT MILLAY

HERBED POTATO SALAD

Serves 6

When you plan to dress potatoes with a vinaigrette rather than a mayonnaise-based dressing, keep the potatoes moist by sprinkling them with olive oil while they are still warm. Make this when the herbs beckon and the potatoes in the markets are new and small.

3 pounds small new potatoes
¼ cup plus 2 tablespoons extra-virgin olive oil
Salt and freshly ground black pepper
3 tablespoons cider or white wine vinegar
3 tablespoons minced shallot
2 cloves garlic, minced
3 tablespoons chopped fresh thyme or chervil
3 tablespoons chopped fresh rosemary
3 tablespoons chopped fresh flat-leaf parsley
1 small red onion, sliced into rings

1. Bring a large pot filled with lightly salted water to a boil over high heat. Halve any potatoes that are longer than 2½ inches. Cook the potatoes for 15 to 18 minutes, or until fork-tender. Drain and shake gently to dry. Transfer the hot potatoes to a large bowl. Sprinkle with about 2 tablespoons of olive oil and season generously with salt and pepper. Set aside to cool to warm room temperature.

2. In a small bowl, whisk together the remaining ¼ cup of oil, the vinegar, shallot, and garlic. Season to taste with salt and pepper. Gently stir in the thyme, rosemary, and 1½ tablespoons of the parsley. Pour the dressing over the room-temperature potatoes and toss gently to mix, taking care not to mash the potatoes. Cover and refrigerate for at least 1 hour, or up to 24 hours until cold.

3. Soak the red onion rings in a shallow bowl of ice water for at least 10 minutes, and up to 1 hour.

4. Lift the onions from the water, shake dry, and scatter over the top of the salad. Sprinkle with the remaining parsley.

FRESH HERBS

herbs can be grown in the garden, or in pots— although most home gardeners and cooks do a little of both. The benefit of pots is that the herbs can be kept on the deck or patio and close to the kitchen. Some, like basil and dill, annuals that you may want a lot of, are best planted in the garden with the vegetables and flowers.

BASMATI RICE SALAD WITH
FRESH PEAS, CORN, AND CHIVES

Serves 6

A room-temperature or cold rice salad is a welcome change from a green salad. It's a satisfying accompaniment for grilled or poached fish or roasted lamb. When peas are ripe in the garden, you can increase the quantity of peas to 2¼ cups and omit the corn. Do the reverse when the sweet corn is at its best.

1½ cups uncooked basmati rice
Pinch of salt

DRESSING:
5 tablespoons white wine vinegar
1 clove garlic, minced
2 teaspoons minced fresh thyme or tarragon
¼ cup extra-virgin olive oil
Salt and freshly ground black pepper

1¼ cups cooked fresh peas
1 cup cooked corn kernels
Grated zest of 1 lemon
6 radicchio leaves (optional)

1. In a medium saucepan, combine the rice, a pinch of salt, and enough cold water to cover by about 1 inch. Bring to a boil over high heat and stir. Cover with a tight-fitting lid, reduce the heat to very low, and cook for about 40 minutes, or until the rice is tender but firm. Check several times while cooking and add more water if the rice is cooking too fast. Remove from the heat, uncover, and let the rice sit for about 5 minutes. Fluff with a fork and set aside to cool to room temperature.

2. To make the dressing: In a small bowl stir together the vinegar, garlic, and thyme. Add the olive oil and whisk until combined. Season to taste with salt and pepper. Cover and set aside.

3. Transfer the rice to a large bowl. Add the peas, corn, and zest and toss to mix. Whisk the dressing and then pour over the salad. Toss gently until all the ingredients are well mixed. Season to taste with salt and pepper. Cover and refrigerate for 30 to 60 minutes. Let the salad return to room temperature before serving.

4. Arrange a radicchio leaf on each of 6 salad plates, if desired. Spoon rice salad onto each leaf and serve.

FRESH CORN: SUMMER GOLD

freshly picked sweet corn is one of the many joys of high summer. Make an effort to buy it from a farmer or stand close to the field where it grows. The natural sugars start to convert to starch from the moment of harvest and the sooner you eat it, the sweeter the corn will taste. It's been said the optimal way to enjoy sweet corn is to put the water on to boil before you dash out to the field to pick the ears!

Tomato and Mixed Basil Salad

Serves 6

Because so many different varieties of basil are grown today—lemon, dark opal, small-leaved bush, and the familiar, green sweet basil, to name a few—we came up with a salad that takes advantage of whatever varieties are thriving in the garden. This salad is deliciously simple. If you have access to red and yellow tomatoes, use both. If not, use one or the other.

6 mixed ripe red and yellow tomatoes (about 3 pounds),
   cut into large cubes
1 medium red onion, thinly sliced
½ cup chopped mixed fresh basil leaves
½ cup extra-virgin olive oil
2 tablespoons red wine vinegar
Salt and freshly ground black pepper

  1. In a large bowl, mix together the tomatoes, red onion, and basil.

  2. In a small bowl, whisk together the olive oil and vinegar. Pour over the salad and toss gently. Season to taste with salt and pepper and serve at once.

CELERY ROOT AND CABBAGE SLAW

Serves 6 to 8

There are numerous ways to make cole slaw. This one, made with celery root, is a refreshing change. Celery root—also known as "celeriac" or "celery knob"—is grown for its large bulbous base rather than for its ribs. Cut off the ends, peel the bulb, and shred it finely in a food processor.

1 celery root, peeled and finely shredded (about 3 cups)
½ small head green cabbage, thinly sliced (about 2 cups)
2 carrots, peeled and finely shredded (about 2 cups)
½ cup finely chopped fresh flat-leaf parsley
2 tablespoons fresh lemon juice
Salt and freshly ground black pepper

DRESSING:
2 tablespoons Dijon mustard
2 tablespoons mayonnaise
2 tablespoons cider vinegar
¼ cup safflower or canola oil
¼ teaspoon ground paprika

Flat-leaf parsley sprigs, for garnish

1. Put the celery root, cabbage, carrots, and parsley in a large bowl. Sprinkle with lemon juice and season generously with salt and pepper. Toss well.

2. To make the dressing: In a small bowl, mix the mustard and mayonnaise together. Stir in the vinegar, and when incorporated, whisk the oil into the mixture until the dressing is creamy and thick, and all of the oil has been emulsified.

3. Pour the dressing over the vegetables and toss well. Add the paprika and toss again. Taste, and adjust the seasonings, if necessary. Serve chilled or at room temperature, garnished with parsley sprigs. If you refrigerate the slaw for several hours, you may want to refresh it with a sprinkling of lemon juice before serving.

Snow Pea–Orange Salad

Serves 6 to 8

Using fresh orange juice as the acid in a vinaigrette is a refreshing change from the more predictable vinegar or lemon juice. Here we use it to dress crunchy snow peas for a lovely, light summer salad.

1 to 1¼ pounds snow peas, trimmed
1 orange, peeled and thinly sliced

Dressing:
2 tablespoons extra-virgin olive oil
2 tablespoons fresh orange juice
1 tablespoon white wine vinegar
1 heaping tablespoon chopped shallot
1 tablespoon chopped fresh thyme
¼ teaspoon chopped grated orange zest
Salt and freshly ground black pepper
3 tablespoons chopped cashews or slivered almonds (optional)

   1. In a saucepan or large skillet, combine the snow peas and water to cover. Bring to a boil over high heat and blanch for about 1 minute. Drain and rinse with cold water. Drain again and pat dry between paper or cloth towels. Transfer the snow peas to a serving bowl and add the orange slices. Toss gently to mix.

   2. To make the dressing: In a small bowl, whisk together the olive oil, orange juice, vinegar, shallot, thyme, and zest. Season to taste with salt and pepper.

   3. Sprinkle several tablespoons of dressing over the salad and toss to coat. Use only enough to moisten. Sprinkle with cashews or almonds, if desired, and serve.

▲

A Buffet Lunch
on the Patio

*vegetable garden
bruschetta*

•

*smoked salmon and
dill deviled eggs*

•

grilled shrimp salad

•

*tomato and mixed
basil salad*

•

snow pea–orange salad

•

*marbled chocolate–
cream cheese brownies*

•

pinot grigio

GRILLED PORTOBELLO MUSHROOM SALAD WITH HERBED GOAT CHEESE

Serves 6

We like the idea of spooning a little herbed goat cheese on the plate next to this mixed salad. The tastes and textures mingle seductively on the tongue. Meaty portobello mushrooms are great for grilling. They aren't really a variety of mushroom, but rather a name given to large cremini mushrooms, which are among the most popular of cultivated culinary mushrooms.

SALAD:

½ cup olive oil
1 clove garlic, crushed
Salt and freshly ground black pepper
2 red bell peppers
1 yellow bell pepper
6 large portobello mushrooms
6 scallions, white and some green parts, sliced

HERBED GOAT CHEESE:

3 ounces mild, fresh goat cheese
2 teaspoons minced fresh thyme
1 teaspoon minced garlic
About 1 teaspoon extra-virgin olive oil
Salt and freshly ground black pepper

DRESSING:

¼ cup balsamic vinegar
½ cup extra-virgin olive oil
Salt and freshly ground black pepper

6 ounces mesclun or other mixed salad greens
  (about 2 loosely packed cups)

1. Prepare a charcoal or gas grill. Lightly spray the grill rack with vegetable oil spray to prevent sticking. The coals should be moderately-hot to hot, and if charcoal, covered with a thin coating of white ash and glowing deep red.

2. In a small bowl, combine the olive oil with the garlic and salt and pepper to taste. Halve the peppers, and stem, seed, and derib them. Cut the peppers lengthwise into quarters and arrange on a large tray or rimmed baking sheet. Trim the stems from the mushrooms and lay the caps on the tray. Lay the scallions on the same tray. Brush the oil over the peppers, mushrooms, and scallions.

3. Grill the peppers for 12 to 15 minutes, turning once, until softened. Lay the peppers on the grill and grill for 8 to 10 minutes, turning once, until lightly charred and softened, and the scallions for 1 to 2 minutes, turning once, until softened. Set the peppers, mushrooms, and scallions aside to cool. Slice the peppers and mushrooms into ½-inch-thick strips. Leave the scallions whole.

4. To prepare the goat cheese: In a small bowl, combine the goat cheese, thyme, and garlic, using a fork to mash the mixture. Drizzle with enough olive oil to moisten the cheese. Season to taste with salt and pepper.

5. To make the dressing: In a small bowl, whisk the vinegar and olive oil together. Season to taste with salt and pepper.

6. In a shallow bowl, combine the lettuce with the grilled peppers, mushrooms, and scallions. Drizzle the dressing over the salad, tossing gently to mix. Use only as much dressing as necessary to moisten the salad. Divide among 6 salad plates. Spoon herbed goat cheese on the side of each plate and serve.

SELECTING FUEL

if you have a charcoal grill, you need to burn charcoal. Many supermarkets and hardware stores sell an astounding array, from standard and self-lighting briquettes to hardwood (or natural) lump charcoal. This last is our choice. Hardwood charcoal burns hotter, longer, and cleaner than others. Some find the irregularly shaped pieces cumbersome, but we think it's a small price to pay. Hardwood lump charcoal is made from woods such as oak, cherry, maple, mesquite, and hickory. It burns nicely, but does not impart flavor. For that, you need smaller wood chunks or chips.

GRILLED SHRIMP SALAD

Serves 6

If you like the Asian flavors of sesame, chile, and citrus, you will enjoy this salad as much as we do. If you especially like sesame, omit the safflower oil in the dressing and replace it with more sesame oil. While the salad makes a good first course, it also makes a refreshingly light meal by itself. Buy jumbo shrimp and leave the tails intact. They are easy to grill and look more appealing, too.

MARINADE:

3 tablespoons safflower oil

2 tablespoons sesame oil

2 tablespoons fresh lime juice

1 small hot red chile, seeded and chopped,
   or 1 to 2 teaspoons red pepper flakes

Freshly ground black pepper

¼ teaspoon coarse salt

12 jumbo shrimp, shelled and deveined, tails attached

DRESSING:

3 tablespoons creamy peanut butter

2 tablespoons soy sauce

3 tablespoons fresh lime juice

2 tablespoons rice wine vinegar

¼ cup dark toasted sesame oil

2 tablespoons safflower oil

SALAD:

8 ounces mesclun or other young greens (6 to 8 loosely packed cups)

3 scallions, green and white parts, thinly sliced on the diagonal

3 or 4 red radishes, thinly sliced

3 tablespoons chopped salted peanuts

2 teaspoons sesame seeds

1. To make the marinade: In a glass or ceramic bowl, stir together the safflower and sesame oils, lime juice, and chile. Season to taste with pepper, and add the salt.

2. Lay the shrimp in a shallow, glass or ceramic dish and pour the marinade over them. Turn to coat. Cover and set aside at room temperature to marinate for no longer than 30 minutes, or refrigerate for no longer than 2 hours.

3. Prepare a charcoal or gas grill. Lightly spray the grill rack with vegetable oil spray to prevent sticking. If using charcoal, let the coals burn until they are hot, covered with a thin layer of white ash, and glowing deep red.

4. Lift the shrimp from the marinade, letting the marinade drip back into the dish. Grill for 2 to 3 minutes. Turn and grill for 2 to 3 minutes longer, or until the shrimp turn pink.

5. To make the dressing: Put the peanut butter in a bowl and whisk until softened. Add the soy sauce and whisk vigorously until smooth. Add the lime juice and vinegar and whisk again. Slowly add the oils, whisking until emulsified.

6. To make the salad: Put the greens in a large bowl. Toss with the scallions and radishes. Spoon a few tablespoons of dressing over the salad and toss until lightly coated. Toss well and then divide the greens among 6 salad plates. Top each plate with 2 shrimp and drizzle with a little remaining dressing. Sprinkle the peanuts and sesame seeds over the salads and serve immediately.

SALAD GREENS

Creating your own mix of young greens insures that your salads will be fresh and delicious. Salad greens can be harvested almost continuously from early spring through early fall. The hottest weeks of July and August are hard on greens, but the rest of the growing season is a delight for them. Mix together an assortment of tender, buttery greens and red leaf and crunchy lettuces. You may not have the space to grow a wide assortment of lettuces, but even a few from your own garden add personality to the salad bowl.

HEIRLOOM TOMATOES

heirloom tomatoes, also called heritage tomatoes or seed-saver tomatoes, are grown from the seeds of varieties not commercially cultivated but instead tended in home gardens and on specialty farms. They may be tiny or large, round or plum shaped, and in hues of red, gold, orange, or yellow. Some are striped. When allowed to ripen in the summer sun before being plucked from the garden, all are sweet, juicy, and delicious. Don't be put off by these glorious fruits if you see them in the market. Try them. You'll like them.

CRABMEAT SALAD WITH HEIRLOOM TOMATOES

Serves 6 to 8

Fresh crabmeat is a luxury worth seeking out. Try quality supermarkets and fish stores for the best lump or backfin crabmeat, already cooked and removed from the shell. It's the ultimate convenience food!

DRESSING:

½ cup mayonnaise
1 tablespoon plus 1 teaspoon fresh lemon juice or white wine vinegar
1 teaspoon Dijon mustard
1 teaspoon finely chopped fresh lemon thyme
*   or regular thyme*
Salt and freshly ground white pepper

SALAD:

1 pound cooked lump or backfin crabmeat
4 medium tomatoes, preferably heirloom varieties,
*   cored and thinly sliced*
Extra-virgin olive oil
Fresh lemon juice
Salt and freshly ground white pepper
Finely minced fresh chives, for garnish (optional)

1. To make the dressing: In a bowl, stir together the mayonnaise, lemon juice, mustard, and thyme. Season lightly with salt and pepper.

2. Using your fingers or a fork, gently break the crabmeat into small pieces. You will have about 4 cups. Add to the bowl and toss gently to . mix with the dressing.

3. Arrange the sliced tomatoes on a serving platter, leaving a space in the middle. Spoon the crabmeat into the center of the platter. Drizzle olive oil and lemon juice over the tomatoes, letting a little get on the crabmeat. Season the tomatoes with salt and pepper. Garnish the crabmeat with chives, if desired, and serve.

HARICOTS VERTS WITH PARSLEY-PECAN PESTO

Serves 6 to 8

We like to make this variation of pesto and toss it with *haricots verts,* the slender French string beans that are available in spring and summer. If you can't find them, use fresh green beans from your garden or from a local farmer. This pesto is also spectacular spooned over grilled chicken, lamb, and fish, or with potatoes, tomatoes, and corn. The keys to success are farm-fresh basil and high-quality, fruity olive oil.

2 cloves garlic, sliced
½ cup pecan halves
¾ cup fresh flat-leaf parsley
¾ cup fresh basil leaves
2 tablespoons fresh lemon juice
¾ cup extra-virgin olive oil
Salt and freshly ground black pepper
2 pounds fresh haricots verts or slim string beans, rinsed and trimmed

   1. Put the garlic, pecans, parsley, basil, and lemon juice in a food processor fitted with the metal blade and process until smooth. With the processor running, slowly pour the olive oil through the feed tube until well blended. Season to taste with salt and pepper.

   2. Bring a large pot of salted water to a boil and cook the beans until just tender, 3 to 5 minutes. Drain immediately and rinse under cold water.

   3. Toss the beans with the sauce, taste, and adjust the seasonings if necessary. Serve slightly chilled or at room temperature.

GRILLED CORN WITH CILANTRO-CUMIN BUTTER

Serves 6

Fresh corn on the cob is one of the many glories of summer. Grilling it, liberally brushed with a garlic and herb butter, makes it especially delicious. Serve this with grilled chicken or steak and plenty of napkins!

½ cup (1 stick) unsalted butter, at room temperature
2 cloves garlic, finely minced
3 tablespoons chopped fresh cilantro
2 tablespoons ground cumin
Salt and freshly ground black pepper
12 ears fresh corn, husked

1. Prepare a charcoal or gas grill. Lightly spray the grill rack with vegetable oil spray to prevent sticking. If using charcoal, let the coals burn until they are hot to medium-hot, covered with a thin layer of white ash, and glowing deep red.

2. Put the butter in a small bowl, add the garlic, cilantro, and cumin, and mash with a fork until mixed. Season to taste with salt and pepper.

3. Brush each ear of corn with the garlic butter. Lay the corn on the grill rack and grill over medium-high heat for 4 to 6 minutes, turning several times, and basting with additional butter, until nicely browned. Just before serving, brush with the remaining butter, season with salt and pepper, and serve at once.

STEAMED MIXED VEGETABLES WITH LEMON-HERB VINAIGRETTE

Serves 6 to 8

We adore oven-roasted or grilled vegetables, but also appreciate the simplicity of steamed vegetables served with a light vinaigrette. The vinaigrette can be prepared well in advance, and you can use any combination of fresh herbs from the garden. Sometimes called "vegetables à la Grecque," this dish can be served warm, cold, or, as we prefer it, at room temperature.

VINAIGRETTE:

1 cup extra-virgin olive oil

¼ cup red wine vinegar

2 tablespoons fresh lemon juice

1 red onion, sliced paper-thin

*2 tablespoons chopped mixed fresh herbs, such as any combination
  of parsley, basil, oregano, thyme, rosemary, and chives*

1 teaspoon salt

½ teaspoon freshly ground white pepper

2 large fennel bulbs, cored and quartered

8 small parsnips, peeled and trimmed

8 baby leeks, rinsed and trimmed

8 baby onions, peeled and trimmed

½ pound green beans, trimmed

1. To make the vinaigrette: In a small bowl, whisk together the olive oil, vinegar, and lemon juice. Stir in the onion, herbs, salt, and pepper. Cover and set aside at room temperature for several hours or overnight. It's convenient to make this in a lidded jar.

continued

extra-virgin olive oil is made by pressing olives without using heat or chemicals, which makes it the most intensely flavored of all olive oils. Depending on the quality of the olives and care taken during pressing, the oil will be fruity and full tasting and may look almost green. On the other hand, many fine extra-virgin olive oils taste mild and refined. Like all good things, a little of this exquisite oil goes a long way, which is why we suggest you use it for salad dressings and for drizzling over vegetables and bread.

2. In a large steamer, steam the fennel for 12 to 15 minutes, or until crisp-tender. Remove from the steamer, set aside, and cover to keep warm. Steam the parsnips for 10 to 12 minutes, the leeks for 8 to 10 minutes, the onions for 8 to 10 minutes, and the greeen beans for 5 to 6 minutes. Be careful not to overcook; all the vegetables should be crisp-tender. When each vegetable is cooked, set it aside, and cover to keep warm.

3. Arrange the vegetables on a large platter, whisk or shake the vinaigrette, and pour it over the vegetables. Serve immediately, while the vegetables are still warm, or let them cool to room temperature. This can also be served chilled.

WARM LENTILS
AND SAUTÉED SPINACH

Serves 6

Lentils are usually considered a wintertime legume, which is too bad, because they are so easy to prepare and taste good all year long. We make this for an early fall lunch in the garden as the clear, cool days of autumn approach.

3 tablespoons olive oil
1½ cups dried lentils
2¼ cups chicken stock, preferably homemade
½ cup water
2 cloves garlic, thinly sliced
10 ounces (1 package) fresh spinach, rinsed, stemmed,
  and coarsely chopped (about 6 cups)
Salt and freshly ground black pepper

   1. Heat 2 tablespoons of the olive oil in a large sauté pan over medium-high heat. Add the lentils and toss to coat with the oil.
   2. Add 2 cups of the chicken stock and the water and bring to a boil. Reduce the heat, cover, and simmer for 25 to 30 minutes, or until the lentils are just tender, stirring occasionally.
   3. Heat the remaining tablespoon of olive oil in another large sauté pan over medium heat. Add the garlic and cook for 1 to 2 minutes, stirring, until tender. Add the spinach and cook, stirring and tossing occasionally, for about 1 minute, until it begins to wilt. Add the remaining ¼ cup of stock and cook until the spinach is tender and completely wilted.
   4. Add the spinach and any cooking liquid to the lentils and toss together. Season to taste with salt and pepper and serve immediately.

desserts & drinks

The more the merrier;
the fewer, the better fare.

—John Palsgrave

SUMMER BERRY SHORTCAKE

Serves 6 to 8

We think berry shortcake is the ultimate early summer dessert. We sprinkle the berries with sugar, but if they are perfectly sweet, there is no need to. Ditto for the whipped cream.

SHORTCAKES:

1¼ *cups unbleached all-purpose flour*

1 cup cornmeal, preferably stone ground

2 tablespoons sugar, plus more for sprinkling

1 tablespoon baking powder

½ *teaspoon baking soda*

½ *teaspoon salt*

6 tablespoons unsalted butter, cut into pieces, chilled

⅔ *cup milk*

1 tablespoon melted butter

BERRIES:

2 pints fresh strawberries

1 pint fresh blueberries

About ¼ cup granulated sugar, or less

1 cup heavy cream

   1. Preheat the oven to 450°F.

   2. To make the shortcakes: In a medium bowl, whisk together the flour, cornmeal, sugar, baking powder, baking soda, and salt. Cut the butter into the flour mixture until it resembles coarse crumbs. Add the milk and stir until the dough holds together.

   3. Turn the dough out onto a lightly floured surface and with floured hands knead 2 or 3 times until cohesive. Pat the dough into a circle ¼ to ½ inch thick. Using a 2½-inch biscuit cutter, stamp out as many biscuits as you can. Put the biscuits on an ungreased baking sheet. Gather the scraps and cut more biscuits.

continued

4. Brush the biscuits with melted butter and sprinkle with sugar. Bake for 11 to 13 minutes until risen and lightly browned. Cool on wire racks.

5. To prepare the berries: Mix the berries in a bowl. Sprinkle with sugar, and toss gently.

6. In the chilled bowl of an electric mixer set on medium-high speed, beat the cream with a whisk until thickened and continue beating until soft peaks form.

7. Split the biscuits and place 2 halves on each plate. Top with berries, a little juice, and several spoonfuls of whipped cream.

SOUR CREAM AND LEMON POUND CAKE WITH WARM RHUBARB SAUCE

Serves 8

This moist and delectable pound cake has a pleasing, crunchy top because of its long baking time. Make it ahead of time, since its flavor improves with a few hours or even a day of "aging."

½ cup (1 stick) unsalted butter, softened
1½ cups sugar
3 large eggs, at room temperature, separated
1¼ cups unbleached all-purpose flour
¼ teaspoon baking soda
⅔ cup sour cream
1 teaspoon pure vanilla extract
1 tablespoon fresh lemon juice
Warm Rhubarb Sauce (recipe follows)

1. Preheat the oven to 325°F. Butter and flour a 9-by-5-inch loaf pan.

2. In the bowl of an electric mixture set on medium-high speed, beat the butter and sugar until smooth and creamy. Add the eggs yolks, one at a time, mixing well after each addition. Continue mixing until the batter is smooth.

3. In a shallow bowl, whisk together the flour and baking soda. Lower the speed of the mixer. Add about a third of the flour to the batter, and beat to incorporate. Add a third of the sour cream and beat again. Add the remaining flour and sour cream to the batter, in alternating thirds. When the batter is smooth, stir in the vanilla and lemon juice.

4. In a clean, dry bowl of an electric mixer fitted with a clean, dry wire whip or beaters, beat the egg whites until stiff peaks form. Using a rubber spatula, fold into the batter. Take care not to overmix the batter, but be sure to incorporate the whites thoroughly. Scrape the batter into the pan and smooth the surface. Bake for about 1 hour and 25 minutes, or until the cake is golden brown, a toothpick inserted in the center comes out clean, and the edges begin to pull away from the sides of the pan.

5. Let the cake cool in the pan set on a wire rack. Serve when cool, cutting the slices directly from the pan, and spooning some of the warm sauce on top. Or cover with plastic wrap or foil and refrigerate for up to 24 hours.

WARM RHUBARB SAUCE

Makes about 2½ cups

We like to take full advantage of rhubarb's short season, early spring through early summer, by making this sauce in batches and freezing it.

3 cups chopped fresh rhubarb (3 to 4 large stalks)
⅓ cup water
⅓ cup crème de cassis
½ cup sugar

1. Put all the ingredients in a large nonreactive saucepan. Bring to a boil over high heat, stirring often. Lower the heat and simmer, uncovered, for 20 to 30 minutes, until the mixture thickens, stirring occasionally. The sauce will be textured.

2. Let the sauce cool slightly in the pan and transfer to a serving bowl. Use immediately, or let tool to room temperature, cover, and refrigerate for 2 to 3 days. The sauce can also be kept frozen for up to 1 month.

▲

SPRINGTIME
DESSERT PARTY
IN THE GARDEN

*sour cream lemon
pound cake with
warm rhubarb sauce*

•

cinnamon ice cream

•

fresh strawberries

•

champagne

ORANGE ANGEL FOOD CAKE WITH FRESH BERRIES AND WHIPPED CREAM

Serves 8 to 10

Light and airy angel food cake is a perfect summertime dessert, and when flavored with a little orange zest, its appeal is heightened. With the addition of mixed berries and whipped cream we turn this simple cake into an elaborate dessert, but you can forgo these and serve it alone or with a scoop of your favorite ice cream.

1½ cups superfine sugar
1 cup unbleached all-purpose flour
½ teaspoon salt
12 large egg whites, at room temperature
1 teaspoon cream of tartar
1½ teaspoons pure vanilla extract
Zest of 1 small orange, finely grated
1 pint fresh raspberries
1 pint fresh blueberries
1 cup heavy cream
Mint sprigs, for garnish

  1. Preheat the oven to 325°F.
  2. In a small bowl, whisk together ½ cup of the sugar with the flour and salt.
  3. In a clean, dry bowl of an electric mixer fitted with a clean, dry wire whip or beaters, beat the egg whites until they are foamy. Sprinkle with cream of tartar, and beat until soft peaks form. Beat in the vanilla and orange zest and the remaining 1 cup of sugar, a tablespoon at a time, and continue beating until the peaks are stiff, but not dry. Using a rubber spatula, fold the flour mixture into the batter. Do not overmix.
  4. Scrape the batter into an ungreased 10-inch tube pan or angel food cake pan. Bake for 50 to 55 minutes, until the cake springs back

continued

when lightly touched. Invert the pan over the neck of a wine bottle, or turn the pan over on it feet. When completely cool, run a kitchen knife around the side of the pan to loosen. Invert the cake onto a platter.

5. While the cake is cooling, toss the raspberries and blueberries in a bowl, cover, and chill until ready to serve.

6. In the bowl of an electric mixer set on high speed, whip the cream until it forms very soft peaks. Cover and chill for at least 1 hour. Serve the cake slices topped with the berries and a large dollop of whipped cream. Garnish each serving with a mint sprig.

BUFFALO BAY APPLE CRISP

Serves 6 to 8

Summer's end, when the first local apples arrive at the farm stands, is the perfect time to make this simple, sweet dessert. The crust tastes like sugar cookies, and it's mixed quickly in a food processor. We prepare it for an annual September pilgrimage to a summer colony on the Connecticut coast called Buffalo Bay. Our friends there have come to look forward to it as an end-of-summer treat.

FILLING:

7 to 8 crisp, tart apples, such as MacIntosh, Cortland,
* Granny Smiths, or Winesaps*
3 tablespoons packed brown sugar
1 to 2 teaspoons ground cinnamon
½ teaspoon ground nutmeg
½ teaspoon ground allspice
2 teaspoons fresh lemon juice

CRUST:

1 cup granulated sugar
1 cup (2 sticks) unsalted butter, softened
1 large egg
2 cups unbleached all-purpose flour

1. Preheat the oven to 350°F.

2. To make the filling: Peel and core the apples. Cut them into slices or large chunks and put in a medium bowl. Add the sugar, cinnamon, nutmeg, and allspice and toss gently to mix. Sprinkle with the lemon juice, toss, and set aside while making the topping.

3. To make the crust: In the bowl of a food processor fitted with the metal blade, combine the sugar and butter. Pulse several times to mix. Add the egg and pulse until combined. Add the flour and pulse until the mixture comes together and forms a cohesive mass.

4. Scrape the apples into a deep dish, such as a 2-quart casserole or large, deep-dish pie plate. Using lightly floured fingers, scoop some of the batter from the food processor and pat into a cookie shape over the apples. Repeat with the remaining batter to make a cobbled crust, with the patties overlapping each other. They should will be relatively thick. Bake for about 1 hour, until the crust is lightly browned and the filling is bubbling around the edges. Let the cobbler cool before serving.

FALL APPLES

the first crisp apples herald cooler weather to come, when we can anticipate a trip to a apple orchard to pick our own. Until then, farm stands and local markets offer lots of local fruit worth seeking out. Although apples are widely grown, the best are from the northern climes, with Washington and New York states yielding the largest crops. Buy fruit with good color and unbroken skin and avoid soft, brown spots. Now is the time for Cortlands, Empires, McIntosh, Northern Spy and other tart, firm apples.

PEAR COBBLER

Serves 6 to 8

Simple, straightforward cobblers rank high with us. Any sort of fruit—
apples, peaches, plums, berries—can be baked into a cobbler. We like to
serve this one in the early autumn, when the first pears appear in the
markets. For a lovely variation, try mixing the pears with apples.

CRUST:

1½ cups sifted unbleached all-purpose flour
¼ teaspoon salt
5 tablespoons unsalted butter, chilled
¼ cup vegetable shortening (such as Crisco), chilled
4 or 5 tablespoons ice water

FILLING:

6 large ripe pears (about ½ pound total weight)
  peeled, cored, and cut into small chunks
1 tablespoon fresh lemon juice
¼ cup sugar, plus 2 tablespoons
½ teaspoon ground ginger
1 tablespoon pear brandy (optional)
2 tablespoons unsalted butter, cut into small pieces

Whipped cream or ice cream, for garnish (optional)

  1. Preheat the oven to 450°F. Lightly butter a deep baking dish,
approximately 7 by 9 inches.
  2. To make the crust: Combine the flour, salt, butter, and shortening
in the bowl of a food processor fitted with a metal blade, and pulse
until the mixture resembles coarse meal. Slowly add the ice water, a
tablespoon or two at a time, and process until the dough begins to hold
together and gathers on the blade. Shape the dough into a ball, working
in a little more flour if necessary. Flatten and wrap in waxed paper or
plastic wrap. Refrigerate for at least 1 hour.

3. To prepare the filling: Put the pears in a large bowl and sprinkle with the lemon juice. Add ¼ cup of the sugar, the ginger, and brandy, if using, and toss together. Set aside at room temperature for about 15 minutes to give juices time to accumulate and sweeten.

4. On a lightly floured surface or on a piece of waxed paper, using a floured rolling pin, roll the dough into a rough 10-by-12-inch rectangle. Line the baking dish with the dough, allowing the excess to hang over the sides.

5. Spoon the pear filling evenly over the dough, sprinkle with the remaining 2 tablespoons of sugar, and dot with the butter. Fold the overhanging dough back over the fruit and pat in place. It will not cover the fruit completely, but will form a decorative edge. Set on the center rack of the oven, and immediately reduce the temperature to 425°F. Bake for about 45 minutes, or until the crust is golden and the fruit is bubbling. Set the pan on a wire rack and allow the cobbler to cool until warm or at room temperature. Serve garnished with whipped cream or ice cream, if desired.

▲

DINNER UNDER
THE STARS

summer borscht

•

*roasted halibut with
parsley-lemon sauce*

•

*steamed mixed
vegetables with
lemon-herb vinaigrette*

•

green salad

•

pear cobbler

•

orvieto

BERRIES

berries are most often associated with summertime. Strawberries in the spring and early summer, blueberries in early summer and midsummer, blackberries in high summer, and raspberries twice, in early summer and early fall. What luck! These growing seasons overlap so that you often can buy two or three kinds of berries at once and toss them together for a colorful, sweet treat. Handle all berries carefully, as they bruise easily, and when you come upon a bumper crop, make jelly and jam.

WARM CRÊPES WITH SUMMER BLUEBERRIES AND PEACHES

Serves 8

We think it's a shame crêpes are not as popular as they once were. This is not a matter of taste—they are great!—but simply a matter of fashion. Try these dessert crêpes, filled with a luscious mixture of blueberries and peaches, a perfect midsummer marriage. Top them with whipped cream, or rich, indulgent crème fraîche, which is available in specialty markets.

CRÊPES:
1 cup milk
2 large eggs, at room temperature, lightly beaten
¼ cup unbleached all-purpose flour
Salt
2 tablespoons unsalted butter

FRUIT FILLING:
3 cups ¼-inch chunks fresh peaches (about 4)
1 cup fresh blueberries
2 tablespoons sugar
½ teaspoon fresh lemon juice
½ teaspoon ground cinnamon

1 cup blueberry preserves

Confectioners' sugar for garnish
Whipped cream or crème fraîche, for garnish

   1. To prepare the crêpes: Whisk the milk and eggs together in a large bowl. Add the flour and salt, whisking until smooth.

   2. Melt ½ teaspoon of the butter in an 8-inch nonstick skillet or crêpe pan over medium heat. When the butter is completely melted, but before it begins to brown, pour about ¼ cup of batter into the center of the pan. Quickly lift the pan off the heat and tip it in several directions so that the batter covers the bottom of the pan.

3. Return the skillet to the heat and cook for 2 to 3 minutes, or until the edges of the crêpe begin to brown. Using a spatula, turn the crêpe and cook for about 1 minute, until lightly browned. Remove the crêpe, and set aside on a plate. Continue cooking crêpes with the remaining batter, adding more butter for each crêpe and stacking them on top of each other as they are cooked. Insert a piece of waxed paper between each freshly made crêpe and the one below. You do not have to keep them warm.

4. Preheat the oven to 400°F. Lightly butter a large baking dish, approximately 9 by 13 inches, or a little larger.

5. To make the fruit filling: Put the peaches and blueberries in a bowl. Add the sugar, lemon juice, and cinnamon, and mix gently.

6. Spoon 2 tablespoons of the fruit mixture into each crêpe and loosely fold the crêpe around the filling. Arrange the crêpes, seam side down, in the baking dish. Bake for about 20 minutes, until heated through.

7. Meanwhile, in a small saucepan, heat the preserves over low heat, stirring occasionally, for about 15 minutes, until warm and bubbly.

8. Place 2 crêpes on each dessert plate. Spoon the warm sauce over them, sprinkle with confectioners' sugar, and top with a dollop of whipped cream or crème fraîche.

FRESH BERRY CROSTADA

Serves 6 to 10

Of all the desserts in this book, this is probably the most elegant.
Mascarpone, a rich, triple-cream fresh cheese, is sold in Italian markets,
specialty shops, cheese shops, and some supermarkets. Mixed with
heavy cream and a little orange liqueur, and spooned into a hazelnut
and cornmeal crust, it makes a dreamy base for the mixed summer
berries scattered on top.

CRUST:

1 cup unbleached all-purpose flour
⅓ cup granulated sugar
¼ cup yellow cornmeal, preferably stone-ground
¼ cup ground hazelnuts
½ teaspoon salt
6 tablespoons unsalted butter, chilled, and cut into pieces
1 teaspoon grated lemon zest
1 large egg, at room temperature, lightly beaten

FILLING:

⅓ cup heavy cream
1 cup mascarpone cheese, at room temperature
¼ cup confectioners' sugar, plus more for dusting
2 tablespoons orange-flavored liqueur
1 cup fresh blackberries
1 cup fresh blueberries
1 cup fresh raspberries

1. To make the crust: Combine the flour, sugar, cornmeal, hazelnuts,
salt, and butter in the bowl of a food processor fitted with a metal blade,
and pulse until the mixture resembles coarse meal. Transfer to a large
bowl and stir in the lemon zest. Add the egg and toss with a fork until
the dough holds together when pressed between your fingertips.

continued

2. Gather into a cohesive mass. Press the dough into the bottom and up the sides of a 10-inch tart pan with a removable bottom. Pierce the bottom of the dough all over with the tines of fork. Cover with plastic wrap, and refrigerate for at least 1 hour or overnight.

3. Preheat the oven to 350°F.

4. Remove the chilled crust from the refrigerator and line it with aluminum foil. Fill with pie weights or dried beans and bake for 20 minutes. Remove the weights and foil. Pierce the crust again in several places to deflate it. Bake for 8 to 10 minutes longer, until lightly browned. Transfer to a wire rack to cool completely.

5. To make the filling: In the bowl of an electric mixer set on high speed, whip the cream with a whire whip or beaters until stiff.

6. In a small bowl, stir together the mascarpone, confectioners' sugar, and liqueur. Fold the whipped cream into the cheese mixture. Spoon into the crust, smoothing the top so that the surface is even. Scatter the berries over the filling and dust with more confectioners' sugar. Remove the sides of the tart pan. Serve immediately, or cover and refrigerate for no longer than 12 hours.

MARBLED CHOCOLATE–CREAM CHEESE BROWNIES

Makes about 2 dozen brownies

These are a nice change from pure chocolate brownies, but are just as easy to make. The marbling dresses them up; the cream cheese gives them richness. Bake these when you are expecting a crowd, and serve them with ice cream or fruit.

4 ounces semisweet chocolate, coarsely chopped
½ cup (1 stick) unsalted butter, softened
3 ounces cream cheese, softened
2½ cups sugar
2 tablespoons heavy cream
1 tablespoon pure vanilla extract
3 large eggs
2 cups unbleached all-purpose flour
1 teaspoon baking powder
¼ teaspoon salt

1. Preheat the oven to 350°F. Butter a 9-by-13-by-2-inch baking pan.

2. Put the chocolate in a microwave-safe measuring cup and microwave on medium (50 percent) power for about 1 minute. Stir and continue microwaving almost 1 minute more or until the chocolate softens and looks shiny. It will not melt completely. Remove the measuring cup from the microwave, and stir the chocolate until smooth. Alternatively, melt the chocolate in the top of a double boiler set over barely simmering water, stirring until smooth. Set aside to cool slightly while preparing the brownie batter.

3. In the bowl of an electric mixer set on medium-high speed, beat the butter, cream cheese, and sugar until smooth. Add the cream and vanilla and beat well. Add the eggs, one at a time, mixing well after each addition, until the batter is smooth.

▲

A SUMMER
AFTERNOON PICNIC

herbed olives
•
*grilled chicken and basil
mayonnaise sandwiches*
•
*tomato and mixed
basil salad*
•
*marbled chocolate–cream
cheese bownies*
•
fresh-squeezed lemonade
•
beer

continued

4. In a shallow bowl, whisk together the flour, baking powder, and salt. Add to the batter, and beat on low speed until incorporated. Scrape the batter into the pan. Pour the melted chocolate over the top of the batter, and using a kitchen knife or rubber spatula, stir the chocolate into the batter with a swirling motion until well marbled.

5. Bake for 25 to 30 minutes, until a toothpick inserted near the center comes out clean and the brownies start to pull away from the sides of the pan. Cool in the pan, set on a wire rack. Cut into squares to serve. Store in an airtight container.

LAURA'S LEMON COOKIES
Makes about 3 dozen cookies

These fragile cookies are light and lemony—perfect for summertime. Serve them with sorbet, ice cream, sliced fruit, iced tea, or lemonade. If you prefer less of a lemon punch, reduce the amount of lemon juice by a tablespoon and a half. These cookies are still soft when taken from the oven, so do not remove them from the baking sheets right away. On the other hand, if they cool on the baking sheets for too long, they will be too crisp to remove. Laura, Mary's daughter, perfected these cookies.

¾ cup (1½ sticks) unsalted butter, softened
1 cup sugar
1 large egg
1¼ cups plus 1 tablespoon fresh lemon juice (about 2 lemons)
1¼ cups unbleached all-purpose flour
Pinch of salt

1. Preheat the oven to 375°F. Butter two baking sheets.
2. In the bowl of an electric mixer set on medium-high speed, cream the butter and sugar for 2 to 3 minutes until light and pale colored. Add the egg and beat for 2 to 3 minutes longer, until creamy. Reduce the speed to medium and beat in the lemon juice.

3. In a shallow bowl, whisk together the flour and salt. With the mixer on low speed, or by hand, gently beat into the batter, mixing just until incorporated.

4. Drop heaping tablespoons of dough onto the baking sheets, leaving at least 1 inch between them. With moistened fingers, smooth the mounds into rounded shapes. Bake for 7 to 8 minutes, until the cookies are just firm in the center and lightly browned around the edges. Remove the baking sheets from the oven, and let the cookies cool on the sheets for no longer than 3 to 4 minutes. Using a metal spatula, carefully transfer the cookies to metal racks to cool completely.

Note: These cookies are fragile and so should be eaten on the day they are baked. They will not keep well for longer than a day or so.

LEMON-LIME SORBET

Serves 6 to 8; makes about 1 quart

Words such as "icy," "refreshing," "cool," and "clean-tasting" will come to mind when you sample this homemade sorbet. It's a light dessert on its own, or serve it with cookies, such as Laura's Lemon Cookies.

1 cup sugar
1½ cups water
¾ cup fresh lemon juice (about 4 lemons)
¾ cup fresh lime juice (4 to 5 limes)
2 teaspoons minced lime zest

1. In a small saucepan, heat the sugar and water over medium heat, stirring occasionally, until the sugar dissolves. Set aside to cool to room temperature. Refrigerate for at least 1 hour, until cold.

2. In a medium bowl, stir together the sugar syrup, lemon juice, lime juice, and zest. Transfer to an ice cream maker. Freeze according to the manufacturer's instructions. Transfer to a metal or plastic container and store in the freezer until ready to serve.

ICED TEA, LEMONADE, AND LIMEADE

Iced teas and lemonade say "summer" as few other beverages do. When made properly, nothing is more refreshing on a hot afternoon or soothing after dinner with dessert. Most people nowadays turn to powdered mixes when making these cooling drinks, which we think is a shame, since the genuine articles are easy and inexpensive to make. Our iced teas are made with mint leaves, lemon verbena, orange pekoe, and cloves, all readily available. For the strawberry tea, you may have to poke around a health food store, although it is in most supermarkets.

Homemade lemonade and limeade require freshly squeezed citrus juice. We recommend making them with sugar syrup, but you can substitute the same amount of sugar, and stir it until dissolved. Fill a tall glass with ice cubes, pour one of these fresh-tasting beverages over them, sit back, and enjoy the garden.

ICED MINT AND LEMON VERBENA TEA

Serves 6

2 quarts water
2 tablespoons mint tea leaves
1 tablespoon plus 1 teaspoon clover honey
8 sprigs lemon verbena
Lemon slices, for garnish

1. Bring the water to a full boil in a large saucepan. Add the tea, and remove the pan from the heat. Cover and let stand for 5 minutes. Add the honey and stir until dissolved. Add the lemon verbena sprigs and let stand for 5 more minutes.

2. Strain into a pitcher and let cool to room temperature. Refrigerate for at least 2 hours. Serve over ice in chilled glasses, garnished with the lemon slices.

ICED ORANGE AND CLOVE TEA

Serves 6

2 quarts water
2 tablespoons plus 2 teaspoons orange pekoe tea leaves
½ cup sugar
6 whole cloves
1 stick cinnamon
Orange slices, for garnish

1. Bring the water to a full boil in a large saucepan. Add the tea, sugar, cloves, and cinnamon stick and remove the pan from the heat. Cover and let stand for 5 minutes. Stir gently to make sure the sugar is dissolved. Let stand for 5 minutes longer.

2. Strain into a pitcher and let cool to room temperature. Refrigerate for at least 2 hours. Serve over ice in chilled glasses, garnished with the orange slices.

ICED STRAWBERRY-LEMON TEA

Serves 6

2 quarts water
2 tablespoons plus 2 teaspoons strawberry tea leaves
½ cup sugar
Juice of 1 lemon
3 large strawberries, sliced, for garnish
Lemon slices, for garnish

1. Bring the water to a full boil in a large saucepan. Add the tea, sugar, and lemon juice, and remove the pan from the heat. Cover and let stand for 5 minutes. Stir gently to make sure the sugar is dissolved. Let stand for 5 minutes longer.

2. Strain into a pitcher and let cool to room temperature. Refrigerate for at least 2 hours. Serve over ice in chilled glasses, garnished with strawberries and lemon slices.

▲

AN AFTERNOON TEA
PARTY FOR FRIENDS

orange angel food cake
with fresh berries
and whipped cream
•
laura's lemon cookies
•
fresh fruit salad
•
lemon-lime sorbet
•
iced orange and clove tea
•
iced strawberry-lemon tea
•
champagne

FRESH-SQUEEZED LEMONADE

Serves 6

1 cup sugar
5½ cups water
1½ cups freshly squeezed lemon juice (about a dozen lemons)
Lemon slices, for garnish

1. Mix together the sugar and ½ cup of the water in a saucepan and bring to a boil over high heat. Reduce the heat, and simmer, stirring with a wooden spoon, for about 5 minutes, until the sugar dissolves. Strain into a lidded glass jar or similar container. Let cool, cover, and refrigerate.

2. Pour the remaining 5 cups of water and the lemon juice into a large pitcher. Add about ¾ cup of the syrup, or more to taste; reserve any remaining syrup for another batch of lemonade. Stir well and pour over ice in tall glasses. Garnish with lemon slices.

SPARKLING LIMEADE

Serves 6

1 cup sugar
½ cup water
1½ cups freshly squeezed lime juice (12 to 14 limes)
1½ bottles (each 1 liter) of club soda or seltzer
Lime slices, for garnish

1. Mix together the sugar and water in a saucepan and bring to a boil over high heat. Reduce the heat, and simmer, stirring with a wooden spoon, for about 5 minutes, until the sugar dissolves. Strain into a lidded glass jar or similar container. Let cool, cover, and refrigerate.

2. Pour the lime juice into a large pitcher. Add about ¾ cup of the syrup, or more to taste; reserve any remaining syrup for another batch of limeade. Stir well and pour over ice in tall glasses. Add club soda to fill the glasses, and stir gently. Garnish with lime slices.

INDEX

A

Apples, 127
  Buffalo Bay Apple Cookie Crisp, 126–27
Asparagus
  Grilled Salade Niçoise with Fresh
    Garden Vegetables, 91–92
  Poached Salmon Salad with Mustard
    Dressing, 86–87
Avocados, 71
  Chilled Avocado Soup, 36
  Chopped Avocado Salad, 71–72

B

Basil, 59
  Fettuccine with Sautéed Cherry
    Tomatoes and Basil, 93
  Grilled Chicken and Basil Mayonnaise
    Sandwiches, 58–59
  Tomato and Mixed Basil Salad, 102
Basmati Rice Salad with Fresh Peas,
  Corn, and Chives, 100–101
Beans
  Black Bean Salsa, 27
  Haricots Verts with Parsley-Pecan
    Pesto, 111
Beef
  Grilled Hamburgers with Red Onion
    Sauce, 60–61
  Spicy Southwestern-Style Grilled Flank
    Steak, 76–77
Beets, 39
  Summer Borscht, 38–39
Bell peppers
  Roasted Red Peppers Stuffed with
    Fresh Corn and Zucchini, 94–95
  Spicy Yellow Tomato Gazpacho, 37–38
Berries, 130. *See also individual berries*
  Champagne-Raspberry Cocktails, 28
  Fresh Berry Crostada, 133–34
  Iced Strawberry-Lemon Tea, 139
  Orange Angel Food Cake with Fresh
    Berries and Whipped Cream, 125–26
  Summer Berry Shortcake, 121–22
  Warm Crêpes with Summer Blueberries
    and Peaches, 130–31
Black Bean Salsa, 27
Blueberries. *See Berries*
Borscht, Summer, 38–39
Bread. *See also Sandwiches*
  Croutons, 37–38
  Grilled Garlic-Herb Bread, 51

Pita Crisps, 17
Rosemary Focaccia, 52–53
Sour Cream Cornbread, 54
Tuna Tartare Toasts, 20
Vegetable Garden Bruschetta, 23
Brownies, Marbled Chocolate–Cream
  Cheese, 135–36
Bruschetta, Vegetable Garden, 23
Buffalo Bay Apple Cookie Crisp, 126–27
Burgers, 60–63

C

Cabbage
  Slaw, Celery Root and, 104–5
Cakes
  Orange Angel Food Cake with Fresh
    Berries and Whipped Cream, 125–26
  Sour Cream and Lemon Pound Cake
    with Warm Rhubarb Sauce, 122–23
Caponata, Roasted Vegetable, 16–17
Celery Root and Cabbage Slaw, 104–5
Champagne-Raspberry Cocktails, 28
Cheese
  Grilled Late-Harvest Pizza, 65–67
  Grilled Portobello Mushroom Salad
    with Herbed Goat Cheese, 106
  Herbed Goat Cheese Spread, 15
  Marbled Chocolate–Cream Cheese
    Brownies, 135–36
  Sour Cream Cornbread, 54
Chicken
  Grilled Chicken and Basil Mayonnaise
    Sandwiches, 58–59
  Grilled Chicken Breasts with Chopped
    Avocado Salad, 71–72
Chocolate–Cream Cheese Brownies,
  Marbled, 135–36
Chowder, Grilled Shrimp and Corn, 44–46
Chutney, Minted Mango, 83
Cobbler, Pear, 128–29
Cocktails, 28–30
Cookies
  Laura's Lemon Cookies, 136–37
  Marbled Chocolate–Cream Cheese
    Brownies, 135–36
Corn, 101
  Basmati Rice Salad with Fresh Peas,
    Corn, and Chives, 100–101
  Corn and Cherry Tomato Salsa, 26–27
  Grilled Corn with Cilantro-Cumin
    Butter, 113
  Grilled Shrimp and Corn Chowder,
    44–46

Roasted Red Peppers Stuffed with Fresh
  Corn and Zucchini, 94–95
Sour Cream Cornbread, 54
Cornish Game Hens, Grilled, with Mint
  Sauce, 73–74
Crab
  Crabmeat Salad with Heirloom
    Tomatoes, 110–11
  Soft-Shell Crab Sandwiches, 56–57
Crêpes, Warm, with Summer Blueberries
  and Peaches, 130–31
Crisp, Buffalo Bay Apple, 126–27
Crostada, Fresh Berry, 133–34
Croutons, 37–38
Cucumbers, 35
  Cool Cucumber Sauce, 62
  Iced Cucumber Soup with Yogurt and
    Dill, 35
  Spicy Yellow Tomato Gazpacho, 37–38

D

Drinks
  alcoholic, 28–30
  nonalcoholic, 138–41

E

Eggplant
  Grilled Late-Harvest Pizza, 65–67
  Roasted Vegetable Caponata, 16–17
Eggs, 22
  Smoked Salmon and Dill Deviled
    Eggs, 22

F

Fennel, 42
  Braised Fennel Soup, 42–43
Fettuccine with Sautéed Cherry
  Tomatoes and Basil, 93
Fish
  Fish Fry with Herbed Tartar Sauce, 88
  Grilled Salade Niçoise with Fresh
    Garden Vegetables, 91–92
  Poached Salmon Salad with Mustard
    Dressing, 86–87
  Roasted Halibut with Parsley-Lemon
    Sauce, 85–86
  Smoked Salmon and Dill Deviled
    Eggs, 22
  Tuna Tartare Toasts, 20
Flowers, edible, 93
Frosty Margaritas, 29

G

Garlic, 51
  Grilled Garlic-Herb Bread, 51
Gazpacho, Spicy Yellow Tomato, 37–38
Grills
  fuel for, 107
  selecting, 63

H

Halibut, Roasted, with Parsley-Lemon
  Sauce, 85–86
Hamburgers, Grilled, with Red Onion
  Sauce, 60–61
Haricots Verts with Parsley-Pecan
  Pesto, 111
Herbs, 98

J

Jersey Tomato Salsa, 24

K

Kabobs, Grilled Pork-and-Pineapple, with
  Scallions, 81–82

L

Lamb
  Grilled Lamb Burgers with Cool
    Cucumber Sauce, 62–63
  Grilled Lamb Chops with Minted
    Mango Chutney, 83
Laura's Lemon Cookies, 136–37
Leeks, 47
  Oyster, Leek, and Scallion Soup, 46–47
Lemons
  Fresh-Squeezed Lemonade, 141
  Iced Strawberry-Lemon Tea, 139
  Laura's Lemon Cookies, 136–37
  Lemon-Herb Vinaigrette, 114–16
  Lemon-Lime Sorbet, 137
  Parsley-Lemon Sauce, 85
  Sour Cream and Lemon Pound Cake
    with Warm Rhubarb Sauce, 122–23
Lentils and Sautéed Spinach, Warm, 117
Limes
  Frosty Margaritas, 29
  Lemon-Lime Sorbet, 137
  Sparkling Limeade, 141
  Vodka-Lime Sea Breezes, 29

M

Mangoes
  Minted Mango Chutney, 83
  Tomato-Mango Salsa, 26

Marbled Chocolate–Cream Cheese
  Brownies, 135–36
Margaritas, Frosty, 29
Menus
  Afternoon Tea Party for Friends, 139
  Al Fresco Pasta Dinner, 53
  Buffet Lunch on the Patio, 105
  Cocktail Party on the Deck, 26
  Dinner on the Porch, 36
  Dinner under the Stars, 129
  Early Autumn Lunch in the Garden, 84
  Early Summer Sunday Lunch, 29
  4th of July Barbecue, 60
  Friday Night Fish Fry, 89
  Late-Summer Lunch in the Garden, 43
  Midsummer Dinner in the Garden, 16
  Santa Fe Supper, 72
  Seafood Lunch for Friends, 57
  Steak on the Grill, 77
  Summer Afternoon Picnic, 135
  Weekend Lunch in the Garden, 94
Mint, 83
  Iced Mint and Lemon Verbena Tea, 138
  Minted Mango Chutney, 83
  Mint Sauce, 73–74
Mushrooms, 79
  Grilled Portobello Mushroom Salad with
    Herbed Goat Cheese, 106
  Grilled Veal Chops with Wild Mushroom
    Sauce, 78–79

O

Olive oil, extra-virgin, 116
Olives
  Herbed Olives, 18
  Roasted Vegetable Caponata, 16–17
Onion Sauce, Red, 61
Oranges
  Iced Orange and Clove Tea, 139
  Orange Angel Food Cake with Fresh
    Berries and Whipped Cream, 125–26
  Snow Pea–Orange Salad, 105
Oysters, 46
  Oyster, Leek, and Scallion Soup, 46–47

P

Parsley, 86
  Parsley-Lemon Sauce, 85
  Parsley-Pecan Pesto, 111
Pasta
  Fettuccine with Sautéed Cherry
    Tomatoes and Basil, 93

Peaches, Warm Crêpes with Summer
  Blueberries and, 130–31
Pear Cobbler, 128–29
Peas
  Basmati Rice Salad with Fresh Peas,
    Corn, and Chives, 100–101
  Cold Minted Pea Soup, 40
Pesto, Parsley-Pecan, 111
Pineapple-and-Pork Kabobs, Grilled, with
  Scallions, 81–82
Pita Crisps, 17
Pizza, Grilled Late-Harvest, 65–67
Pork-and-Pineapple Kabobs, Grilled, with
  Scallions, 81–82
Potatoes
  Grilled Salade Niçoise with Fresh
    Garden Vegetables, 91–92
  Herbed Potato Salad, 99

R

Raspberries. *See* Berries
Red Onion Sauce, 61
Rhubarb Sauce, Warm, 123
Rice Salad, Basmati, with Fresh Peas,
  Corn, and Chives, 100–101
Rosemary Focaccia, 52–53

S

Salads, 109
  Basmati Rice Salad with Fresh Peas,
    Corn, and Chives, 100–101
  Celery Root and Cabbage Slaw, 104–5
  Chopped Avocado Salad, 71–72
  Crabmeat Salad with Heirloom
    Tomatoes, 110–11
  Grilled Portobello Mushroom Salad with
    Herbed Goat Cheese, 106
  Grilled Salade Niçoise with Fresh
    Garden Vegetables, 91–92
  Grilled Shrimp Salad, 108
  Herbed Potato Salad, 99
  Poached Salmon Salad with Mustard
    Dressing, 86–87
  Scallop Seviche, 21
  Snow Pea–Orange Salad, 105
  Tomato and Mixed Basil Salad, 102
Salmon
  Poached Salmon Salad with Mustard
    Dressing, 86–87
  Smoked Salmon and Dill Deviled
    Eggs, 22
Salsas, 24
  Black Bean Salsa, 27

Corn and Cherry Tomato Salsa, 26–27
Jersey Tomato Salsa, 24
Tomato-Mango Salsa, 26
Sandwiches, 56–63
Sauces
  Cool Cucumber Sauce, 62
  Herbed Tartar Sauce, 89
  Mint Sauce, 73–74
  Parsley-Lemon Sauce, 85
  Parsley-Pecan Pesto, 111
  Red Onion Sauce, 61
  Tarragon-Mustard Sauce, 84
  Warm Rhubarb Sauce, 123
  Wild Mushroom Sauce, 78–79
Sausages, Mixed Grill of, with Tarragon-
  Mustard Sauce, 84
Scallions
  Grilled Pork-and-Pineapple Kabobs
    with Scallions, 81–82
  Oyster, Leek, and Scallion Soup, 46–47
Scallop Seviche, 21
Shortcake, Summer Berry, 121–22
Shrimp
  Grilled Shrimp and Corn Chowder,
    44–46
  Grilled Shrimp Salad, 108–9
Slaw, Celery Root and Cabbage, 104–5
Snow Pea–Orange Salad, 105
Soft-Shell Crab Sandwiches, 56–57
Sorbet, Lemon-Lime, 137
Soups
  Braised Fennel Soup, 42–43
  Chilled Avocado Soup, 36
  Cold Minted Pea Soup, 40
  Grilled Shrimp and Corn Chowder,
    44–46
  Iced Cucumber Soup with Yogurt and
    Dill, 35
  Oyster, Leek, and Scallion Soup, 46–47
  Spicy Yellow Tomato Gazpacho, 37–38
  Summer Borscht, 38–39
Sour Cream and Lemon Pound Cake with
  Warm Rhubarb Sauce, 122–23
Sour Cream Cornbread, 54
Sparkling Limeade, 141
Spinach, Sautéed, Warm Lentils and, 117
Spreads, 15–17
Strawberries. See Berries
Summer Berry Shortcake, 121–22
Summer Borscht, 38–39
Summer Sangria, 30

T
Tarragon-Mustard Sauce, 84
Tartar Sauce, Herbed, 89
Tea
  Iced Mint and Lemon Verbena Tea, 138
  Iced Orange and Clove Tea, 139
  Iced Strawberry-Lemon Tea, 139
Tomatoes, 27, 110
  Corn and Cherry Tomato Salsa, 26–27
  Crabmeat Salad with Heirloom
    Tomatoes, 110–11
  Fettuccine with Sautéed Cherry
    Tomatoes and Basil, 93
  Grilled Late-Harvest Pizza, 65–67
  Grilled Salade Niçoise with Fresh
    Garden Vegetables, 91–92
  Grilled Shrimp and Corn Chowder,
    44–46
  Jersey Tomato Salsa, 24
  Roasted Vegetable Caponata, 16–17
  Spicy Yellow Tomato Gazpacho, 37–38
  Tomato and Mixed Basil Salad, 102
  Tomato-Mango Salsa, 26

Vegetable Garden Bruschetta, 23
Tuna
  Grilled Salade Niçoise with Fresh
    Garden Vegetables, 91–92
  Tuna Tartare Toasts, 20

V
Veal Chops, Grilled, with Wild Mushroom
  Sauce, 78–79
Vegetables. See also individual
vegetables
  Grilled Late-Harvest Pizza, 65–67
  Roasted Vegetable Caponata, 16–17
  Steamed Mixed Vegetables with
    Lemon-Herb Vinaigrette, 114–16
  Vegetable Garden Bruschetta, 23
Vodka-Lime Sea Breezes, 29

Z
Zucchini, 95
  Roasted Red Peppers Stuffed with Fresh
    Corn and Zucchini, 94–95

TABLE OF EQUIVALENTS

The exact equivalents in the following tables
have been rounded for convenience.

OVEN TEMPERATURES			WEIGHTS		LIQUIDS		
Fahrenheit	Celsius	Gas	US/UK	Metric	US	Metric	UK
250	120	½	1oz	30g	2tbl	30ml	1fl oz
275	140	1	2oz	60g	¼ cup	60ml	2fl oz
300	150	2	3oz	90g	⅓ cup	80ml	3fl oz
325	160	3	4oz (¼lb)	125g	½ cup	125ml	4fl oz
350	180	4	5oz (⅓lb)	155g	⅔ cup	160ml	5fl oz
375	190	5	6oz	185g	¾ cup	180ml	6fl oz
400	200	6	7oz	220g	1 cup	250ml	8fl oz
425	220	7	8oz (½lb)	250g	1½ cup	375ml	12fl oz
450	230	8	10oz	315g	2 cups	500ml	16fl oz
475	240	9	12oz (¾lb)	375g	4 cups/1qt	1l	32fl oz
500	260	10	14oz	440g			
			16oz (1lb)	500g			
			1½lb	750g			
			2lb	1kg			
			3lb	1.5kg			